Thankful for all of those who have had Faith in The FATHER and allowed HIM to lead them out of their own thoughts and feelings.

Thankful that HE saw me worthy and deemed me a Child of The KING! HalleluYAH!

Thankful for the Total, Complete and Finished work of YESHUA, JESUS The CHRIST on The Cross on Calvary.

Thankful for my mother, and her remaining by my side through it all! Also, very proud of her growth on this path and in this process from Glory to Glory. AMen

This book is dedicated to my brother Lee G. Wilson. Your life was a Blessing and your memory is a treasure. You are Loved beyond words and missed beyond measure!

We talked about these methods many times. We discussed the truth of them and how "spot on" they are.

Only one who understands the turmoil and captivity of addiction, vices, strongholds, and deception can see that as clearly as we did bro!

I Love & Miss You Lee!

Lee George Wilson
03.12.1965-02.04.2019

A GUIDE

RESIDUE:
Remove Every Stronghold In-Depth. Undo Everything!

By David Arthur

Table of Contents

It is highly suggested and recommended that every person that takes part of The RESIDUE Guide will have a KJV or NASB Bible handy, a journal or large notebook as well as the appropriate writing utensils.

The RESIDUE Guide is best done with a group of 2 or more. Men must gather with men while women gather with women. It is important to keep the groups separated while taking part of this process.

IBA Ministries
PO Box 172
Hancock, ME. 04640

www.ibelongAmen.com

Introduction to R.E.S.I.D.U.E.

Remove

Every

Stronghold

In-

Depth!

Undo

Everything!

My name is David, and I fought a lonely, almost losing battle with sexual brokenness, among many other strongholds, habits, and addictions. For over 30 years I was so lost and so broken, hurting and delirious before I was rescued by JESUS The CHRIST and was able to find that there truly is Hope and help on the way to Absolute Freedom from any stronghold, any addiction and any sin. Although my identity was found in my thoughts and feelings it was also learned through culture and society. I've finally discovered my True Identity as it is being revealed to me.

YAHWEH, GOD Almighty, is able to bring good out of bad! HE is able to bring good out of misery. HE is able to do exceedingly and abundantly more than any of us could ever think or imagine.

Working these 6 methods, and closely observing the Purpose for each Method, along with understanding the biblical Truth regarding Intimacy and our design, makes it so that sinful activity ceases and the power of temptation lessens.

There is no quick fix or easy solution. JESUS is not some magic pill! I still have times of fleshly struggle, but the Good Shepherd has found HIS wandering sheep, has me on HIS shoulder, and HE is carrying me Home! HalleluYAH!

It is not that I do not struggle, but that I do not struggle with my struggle because I can be confident, secure, safe and content in the finished, total and complete work of JESUS The CHRIST on The Cross.

GOD'S Word shows how this Freedom is available to every single one of us. The Bible tells us how we can have HIS enabling power in our lives so that we can follow HIS Counsel and come to realize HIS Promise to be with us has already been fulfilled in JESUS The CHRIST, now we must acknowledge and accept this reality.

Each of the 6 methods is a guide that can help us to know and to recognize GOD'S Strength in and during our struggles. The methods and purposes show us how lives can be changed; lives that were ineffectual and unhappy into lives that are Joyful and Fruitful.

We have used the KJV and NASB versions making this booklet.

1. Can the Bible show me how to find Freedom?

Joshua 1:8 ~ [8] This book of the law [instruction] shall not depart from your mouth, but you shall meditate on it day and night, so that you may be careful to do according to all that is written in it; for then you will make your way prosperous, and then you will have success.

Well, gaining knowledge of the Bible is vital to discovering our true identity, but it is only when the Truth of Scripture becomes part of the very core of our being that it can do it's transforming work. When Scripture is rooted in our very souls it is then that an immeasurable power is released! Don't believe me? Try it!

There is a story I once read….. One day in 1945, Clarence W. Hall, a war correspondent following on the heels of our troops in Okinawa, came upon the tiny village of Shimabuku. It was an obscure little community of only a few hundred native Okinawans. Now 30 years before, an American missionary on his way to Japan, had stopped here. He had not stayed long, just long enough to make a few converts, leave them a Bible, and move on.

One of the converts was Shosei Kina; the other his brother Mojon. From the time of the missionary's visit they had seen no other missionary and had had no contact with any other Christian person. In those 30 years Shosei Kina and his brother had made their New Testament come alive. Aflame with their discovery, they taught the other villagers until every man, woman and child in Shimabuku had become a Child of GOD. Shosei Kina became head man in the village; his brother, Mojon, the chief teacher.

In Mojon's school the Bible was read daily. To Shosei Kina's village government, The Bible's precepts were law. Under the impact of this book, pagan practices fell away. In their place there had developed a Christian democracy at its purest.

After 30 years came the American army, storming across the island. Little Shimabuku was directly in its path and took some severe shelling. When our advance patrols swept up to the village compound, the GIs, guns leveled, stopped dead in their tracks as two little old men stepped forth, bowed low and began to speak. An interpreter explained that the old men were welcoming them as fellow Christians. They remembered that their missionary had come from America. So, though these Americans seemed to approach things a little differently, the two old men were overjoyed to see them.

The GIs reaction was typical. Flabbergasted, they sent for the chaplain. The chaplain came, and with him the officers of the Intelligence Service. They toured the village and were astonished at what they saw--spotlessly clean homes and streets, poised and gentle villagers, a high level of health and happiness, intelligence, and prosperity. They had seen many other villages on Okinawa--villages of unbelievable poverty and filth. Against these Shimabuku shone like a diamond in a dung heap.

Shosei Kina and his brother Mojon observed the American's amazement and took it for disappointment. They bowed humbly and said, "We are sorry if we seem a backward people. We have, honored sirs, tried our best to follow the Bible and live like JESUS. Perhaps if you will show us how."

Hall relates that he strolled through Shimabuku one day with a tough old Army sergeant. As they walked the sergeant turned to him and whispered hoarsely, "I can't figure it--this kind of people coming out of only a Bible and a couple of old guys who wanted to live like Jesus!" Then he added a penetrating observation: "Maybe we've been using the wrong kind of weapons."

Psalm 119:9 – [9] How can a young man keep his way pure? By keeping *it* according to Your word.

> "This book [The Bible] will keep you from sin, or sin will keep you from this book." ~ D. L. Moody

Psalm 119:11 - [11] Your word I have treasured in my heart, that I may not sin against You.

Psalm 119:105 – [5] Oh that my ways may be established to keep Your statutes!

One of our largest hurdles in the healing process is our own obsession with instant and immediate results. This 'itch' riddles our thinking so that we actually begin to think that unless healing is instant, then it must not be possible, or even 'of GOD'. We have become very impatient and get frustrated with anything that actually takes time. Dare I say, 'entitled'.

Isaiah 8:20 – [20] To the law and to the testimony: if they speak not according to this word, it is because there is no light in them.

Since the Word of God can do so much for us, it is not surprising that the enemy of our souls would try to turn us away from it. For this reason, both Old and New Testaments are full of warnings against false prophets and fake teachers.

"We are to receive nothing for truth but what is agreeable to the Word. As God has given to his ministers gifts for interpreting obscure places, so he has given to his people so much of the spirit of discerning, that they can tell (at least in things necessary to [the hope of eternal] salvation) what is consonant to Scripture, and what is not. We have this blessed Book of God to resolve all our doubts, to point out a way of life to us. God having given us his written Word to be our directory takes away all excuses of men. No man can say, I went wrong for want of light; God has given thee his Word as a lamp to thy feet; therefore, if thou goest wrong, thou does it willfully. The Spirit of God acts regularly, it works in and by the Word; and he that pretends to a new light, which is either above the Word, or contrary to it, abuses both himself and the Spirit: his light is borrowed from him who transforms himself into an angel of light (Satan)." ~ Thomas Watson

One of the biggest lies in this world is that old party line of 'They Say'; They Say you're born that way. They Say it is a disease. They Say it is an attraction. They Say you're worthless. They Say and they say and they say.... but know The Truth.

John 8:31-32 – [31] Then said Jesus to those Jews which believed on him, If ye continue in my word, then are ye my disciples indeed; [32] And ye shall know the truth, and the truth shall make you free.

People will go to a lot of trouble to learn another language or how to do hair, become a barber or build a computer, even how to operate a cb radio. They have the patience to learn how to operate a car, or a semi-truck, but can't be bothered learning how to operate themselves according to GOD'S GOoD & Perfect Word/Will.

It is okay to struggle with something! It is okay to struggle because that means we recognize that it is a struggle. Overcoming our struggles takes a lot of work, a lot of prayer and we must be reprogrammed, thus becoming new creations. Our old characteristics and nature must go! Our old mannerisms must change! Much of this work can, and should, be done with brothers and sisters for support and also for accountability.

2Timothy 3:16-17 – [16] All scripture is given by inspiration of God, and is profitable for doctrine, for reproof, for correction, for instruction in righteousness: [17] That the man of God may be perfect, thoroughly furnished unto all good works.

Our minds are stuck in a rut, a pattern of thinking that is antagonistic to the will of God. Successful Christian living depends on getting out of that rut and establishing another one that is characterized by biblical values and ways of thinking.

We are all where we are, and we have all become what we are, due to our own choices! It is our fault. No blaming the devil here. We have not protected, or considered what we allow to enter, our eyes and ears! We have allowed much darkness into our minds and into our hearts. If we are ever going to change then we had better start paying attention to what we watch, listen to, speak of, speak on, and all that we allow into our hearts and our homes.

It is time that we begin to change our habits and become the men and women of GOD that we were intended to be. This is no longer "personal", it has now become an "intimacy" issue. I know that many like the old saying, "I have a personal relationship with GOD" and as wonderful as that may sound, or as great as it may make you feel, if you have a "personal" relationship with GOD, then you have created your own god and that is the god you worship.

Once we surrender to HIM, it is no longer personal! It has gone from personal to Intimate. We become an exceedingly small part of a great big body. Now we have an Intimate relationship with The FATHER and that is what HE desires of us. So, let us recognize the difference between personal relations and intimate ones. We must be intimately intertwined for the body to function properly.

At this time, please consider what you've read and learned, and journal your own personal response to this. This can be of great help in the future to see how you are progressing and changing.

2. Will GOD help me understand HIS Truth?

Psalm 25:8 – [8] Good and upright is the LORD: therefore will he teach sinners in the way.

Psalm 32:8-9 – [8] I will instruct thee and teach thee in the way which thou shalt go: I will guide thee with mine eye. [9] Be ye not as the horse, or as the mule, which have no understanding: whose mouth must be held in with bit and bridle, lest they come near unto thee.

A man was walking behind a gypsy woman and when they came to a place where the road divided, the woman threw her stick up into the air, and let it fall on the ground. Then she did it a second time; and a third.

By this time the gentleman had caught up with her, and, being curious, he asked: 'Why do you throw your stick up into the air like that?'

She replied, 'That is how I determine which way to go; I go whichever way the stick points.'

'But you threw it up three times,' he said, wondering why she had done so.

'Yes, I did!' she answered, 'for the silly thing pointed that way, and I want to go this way!'

We may smile, or chuckle, at that woman's ignorance, but are we any wiser when we do not let YESHUA, JESUS The CHRIST, have the reins, while we only obey HIS Commands if they agree with our own wants, thoughts or feelings?

We must allow JESUS to be LORD and SAVIOR of, in, with, through and over our lives!

And remember, The HOLY SPIRIT will never point to HIMSELF, nor will HE ever point to you. HE will always point to The Cross and HE will never take you outside of The Word of GOD. Ever!

At this time, please consider what you've read and learned, and journal your own personal response to this. This can be of great help in the future to see how you are progressing and changing.

3. What should my attitude be for maximum benefit?

Psalm 86:11 – [11] Teach me thy way, O LORD; I will walk in thy truth: unite my heart to fear thy name.

We cannot walk in The Way, GOD'S Way, unless HE teaches us, but it is silly and ignorant to ask HIM to teach us unless we truly decide to obey HIM as HE instructs us. To do that we need what the psalmist prayed for, a heart united in reverence for HIM.

Psalm 119:18 – [18] Open thou mine eyes, that I may behold wondrous things out of thy law.

Dependence on the Holy Spirit to teach us will guard us against placing too much confidence in ourselves and failing to trust the Lord for needed understanding. Of course, dependence on the Holy Spirit does not mean that study is unnecessary.

GOD may sometimes quickly give us an understanding of a particular passage, while at other times we may have to study patiently [and diligently] for insight.

At this time, please consider what you've read and learned, and journal your own personal response to this. This can be of great help in the future to see how you are progressing and changing.

<u>Method</u>

1. Accept that we are powerless and in bondage, while admitting to GOD only (for now) our deepest darkest secrets.

2. See the purpose in our suffering and out failures. We learn from it.

3. Accept the fact that our intended identity is found only, in YESHUA, JESUS The CHRIST.

4. Create an extremely transparent and very humbling moral inventory.

5. Admit to others, those deepest darkest secrets that were confessed to GOD, and relate to our moral inventory.

6. Make an amends, when possible/appropriate, to the people we have harmed, hurt, used and abused.

Purpose

1. To release the power they hold over us. Know & Believe we are Forgiven regardless of all that we have done and had or have become.

2. To know that we have been deceived, a deception that trapped us in a false identity.

3. To be able to Trust our FATHER in Heaven, confident that it will bring us into a familiar and familial bond with HIM, and our brethren (brothers & sisters). Intimacy!

4. & 5. Are very closely related and are both needed in this order. We write down this moral and very convicting inventory to reveal to us exactly who and what we are and had become. We utilize this inventory in Method 5 to help us when we admit (confess) to others, those deepest darkest secrets that we confessed to GOD Alone.

6. Forgiveness. This is not just for us; it is for all involved.

Method 1. Accept that we are powerless and in bondage, while admitting to GOD only (for now) our deepest darkest secrets.

Purpose 1. To prepare ourselves to release the power those deep dark secrets hold over us. To know & Believe we are Forgiven regardless of all that we have done and had or have become.

In method 1 we acknowledge that we are powerless over the lusts of our flesh and that we can do nothing by our own strength. By doing so, we gain the humility we need to reach out to our One, True Living GOD, YAHWEH, and to others (HIS Own) for the help we must have if we are to experience the glorious liberty of discovering our true identity.

Method 1 has a total of 21 questions. Please be patient and do not try to rush it, because it does not work if we do not truly work on each section/question and apply it to our lives.

How long and how cleverly we defended our right to wrong ourselves and others by denying that there was anything wrong at all. Some of us fooled ourselves by claiming that there was nothing really wrong because we only engaged in wrong activity "once in a while". Some of us just rationalized our behavior in many other ways. And maybe many of us saw nothing wrong with what we were doing, or did we?!

I ignored the facts that fleshly desires like pornography, being promiscuous and/or masturbation ruled my life just as much as drugs, cigarettes, anger, jealousy, alcohol and many other strongholds did.

When it comes to sexual brokenness, especially the sin of homosexuality, many of us have been misled to believe that we were created that way or that it is okay, and it is 'normal' and so we lived some very dark and destructive lives. I know how it became my entire identity, my world, every single fiber of my being.

My identity in homosexuality and transgenderism ruled my thoughts, feelings, actions, and life! It determined my friends. It determined which of my blood relatives I associated with. It determined where I lived, partied, hung out and what businesses I would frequent.

No matter what our stronghold or addiction, some of us have tried to quit. Failing that, we sought to cut down. We made promises and plans, but to no avail. We summoned up all our will-power, only to fail repeatedly. Thus, believing that there was just nothing we could possibly do. And in a way, we were right, because 'we' can't do it without HIS Strength.

Many of us could not control our outward behavior. The rest of us could not calm the fierce war raging within us. How can we even begin to understand something if we have already been programmed with what it is?

What we did not express with the body of another, or our own body, we expressed by diving deeper into very destructive behavior leaving us guilty, ashamed, frightened, and hopeless.

Our despair was so oppressive that some of us have even thought about taking, or have tried to take, our own lives.

And so, we faced the truth that the pain and the hurt we were causing ourselves, and others, was too real, and too intense, to ignore. We were compelled to admit, "Something is desperately wrong. I have a real problem, and I cannot solve it on my own." Strangely, this admission of being *powerless* is our first step to Strength.

Our confession of slavery started us on the road that leads to Freedom! Freedom is found in becoming a bond-servant.

We are first going to go over the GOD Ordained sexuality to cover all bases carefully. The goal is to understand who and what we were Created to be, GOD'S Design. YAHWEH, GOD Almighty, intended our identity to be found in HIS Only Begotten Son, JESUS The CHRIST.

However, the fall of man hindered that intention, but only until we understand HIS intention and Creation. Please be patient and learn the basics as we all journey this discovery process together.

Created in the image of GOD. Born in the image of Adam.

Born into and shaped in iniquity.

1. What sexual activity was ordained by GOD?

Genesis 2:24 ~ For this reason a man shall leave his father and his mother, and be joined to his wife; and they shall become one flesh.

Genesis 2:24 is clear that one man is to be joined to one woman and that the two become one flesh. "One Flesh" is very important.

Man was Created, woman was formed from "the rib" of man. Whether that is symbolic or literal, it doesn't change the fact that only one man and one woman can become "One Flesh" when the rib is rejoined to its rightful place, thus the two becoming One Flesh.

Two ribs (two women) cannot become One Flesh, neither can two males each missing the rib. So, same sex marriage is not recognizable in the eyes of GOD. It is important we desire to see through HIS lens.

At this time, please consider what you've read and learned, and journal your own personal response to this. This can be of great help in the future to see how you are progressing and changing.

2. Did JESUS think that which was originally ordained should be weakened or abandoned in any way?

Matthew 19:4-5 ~ [4] And He answered and said, "Have you not read that He who created *them* from the beginning MADE THEM MALE AND FEMALE, [5] and said, 'FOR THIS REASON A MAN SHALL LEAVE HIS FATHER AND MOTHER AND BE JOINED TO HIS WIFE, AND THE TWO SHALL BECOME ONE FLESH'?

The biblical case against practicing homosexuality rests on the constant, pervasive biblical teaching that sex is a gift intended for the committed relationship of a man and a woman in a life-long covenant. Never is there a hint anywhere in Scripture that GOD intended sex in any other relationship."

A man may have sexual relations with a woman who is married to him; with a woman who is married to someone else; with a woman who is unmarried; or with another man. The Bible condemns the last three--adultery, fornication, and homosexual practices--in no uncertain terms, and is equally definitive in approving the first.

At this time, please consider what you've read and learned, and journal your own personal response to this. This can be of great help in the future to see how you are progressing and changing.

3. Does the Bible teach that homosexuality is contrary to GOD'S Will or HIS Design?

In Genesis 1 and 2 we clearly see GOD'S intention, mankind as male and female. The fall of man distorts that intention and then the law arises in response to the deviation from GOD'S good intent.

Is it any wonder why, although sin is sin and in GOD'S eyes if we are guilty of just one transgression then we are guilty of all transgressions, homosexuality is not "just another sin"?

This is so because homosexuality is a direct and deliberate attack on GOD'S very thought of Creation as one male and one female, becoming One Flesh.

Understand this, murderers know that it is wrong to take a life. And although some of them feel as if their actions are justifiable, that doesn't change the fact that they know it is wrong to murder.

If you catch a thief red-handed then he will almost always be repentant and beg for forgiveness, or at least apologize for his wrong. Why? Because he knows it is wrong.

A man that is cheating on his wife doesn't walk his mistress through the town square or take her to a family reunion but rather hides away in some seedy hotel or out in the woods in the backseat of a car because of his own convictions of what is right and what is wrong. He knows adultery is wrong.

A man lusting after another man's wife doesn't tell the husband of the woman he is lusting after because we all know, deep within, what is right and what is wrong.
The homosexual movement had me, and many others still, out in the streets marching and parading for extra or special rights just because of our sexual preference.

Note I said preference, not orientation. Our sexual preference can vary and is determined on our thoughts and feelings, however, our GOD-Given heterosexual design cannot be changed or altered although it can be denied and refused.

"...the law appears as an agent of reconciliation directing sinful man to CHRIST." ~ A. Comiskey

Leviticus 18:22-24 ~ [22] You shall not lie with a male as one lies with a female; it is an abomination. [23] Also you shall not have intercourse with any animal to be defiled with it, nor shall any woman stand before an animal to mate with it; it is a perversion [24] 'Do not defile yourselves by any of these things; for by all these the nations which I am casting out before you have become defiled.

These words made many of us angry because we thought GOD was being inconsistent or tyrannical, like a parent who says, "You can't wear blue just because I don't like it." GOD is neither of those things. GOD is Love (1John 4:16).

When HE tells us not to walk in a certain way, it is because HE knows that that road will be destructive and even deadly for some of us not only physically but emotionally and spiritually as well.

Unfortunately, our instinctual sex drive, which has been joined to deep emotional needs for love (a desire for intimacy) when we were young (for many), makes us like people lost in a snow storm.

We have tried to fight our way out but are now so weary that the snow looks warm and inviting. If only we can lie down and just go to sleep, all will be well. To do so feels good, but to do so is to die! And so, our Almighty FATHER lovingly urges us not to give in, but to fight on, promising Freedom to those who will Trust HIM and just surrender.

Romans 1:26-27 ~ ²⁶ For this reason God gave them over to degrading passions; for their women exchanged the natural function for that which is unnatural, ²⁷ and in the same way also the men abandoned the _natural function_ of the woman and burned in their desire toward one another, men with men committing indecent acts and receiving in their own persons the due penalty of their error.

Some of us were deeply troubled by these words. We thought GOD had somehow selected us for special condemnation. We failed to read these words in their proper context.

What the passage is saying is that all men who have turned away from GOD to things they chose to worship are sinners. GOD then let them do what they wanted to do. Some were given over to various sins (Romans 1:24-25); others to the sin of homosexuality (Romans 1:26-27); others to other sins (Romans 1:28-31). "All have sinned and come short of the Glory of GOD" (Romans 3:23).

We are all worthy of death (Romans 1:32)! All of us are in the same boat! We only sit on different planks!

Let's look at the two words that stood out to me from Romans 1:26-27; "natural" and "function".

Paul was very wise and led by The Spirit of The One True Living GOD, when he used these two words. What comes 'natural' to us in our fallen state (born into sin/shaped in iniquity) is much different than what comes natural to us after we get Saved. At least it does in time as we begin the process of sanctification, and as discernment and conviction begin to take hold.

The one thing that does not change in our fallen state or our saved state is our function. Our function never changes, it always remains the same. Even when we don't know it, recognize it, or deny it.

We all naturally have a sex organ that naturally fits with the sex organ of the opposite sex. Our function, then is to become One Flesh and to procreate.

GOD tells us we are sinners to show us our need of the Forgiveness (Romans 3:21-5:21) and The Freedom (Romans 6:1-8:39) for which YESHUA, JESUS The CHRIST, died on The Cross.

Romans 1:26-27 was not written to harm us, but to bring us to HIM. It is motivated by a Love which sacrificed everything for us and is written that we might enjoy the Blessings of that sacrifice. Our all-knowing, all-loving GOD Loves us so very much that HE robed HIMSELF in flesh, came to Earth and became the propitiation for our sins!

GOD Almighty became the payment, the ransom, for your wrongs you've done unto HIM.

Ever heard that old saying, "If you love someone let them go. If they return it was meant to be."? Well our Loving FATHER Loves us so much that HE has let us go in order to find us, because we must discover our true identity in JESUS. It is through our suffering and anguish (all due to our own choices) that we return to HIM.

We don't "find JESUS" because JESUS isn't the one who is lost. HE finds us! We are the lost ones. There is Freedom in HIM!

However, when GOD "gives us up to our sin" as "reprobates", HE is therefore releasing us completely to our sins that we choose over HIM.

But only HE knows who is given up to their sin. Only HE knows who a reprobate is. We do not! Many called me a reprobate when I was a transgender prostitute, addict and criminal. Yet here I stand as a Forgiven and Free Bond-Servant of CHRIST! AMen!!

We must carry on HIS Message of the Hope of an eternal salvation that is available to every single person we encounter. HE Wills that all men be saved! All means all!

I know you've heard many ideas and thoughts and feelings and so on about homosexuality and all of the confusion that stems from that brokenness, but please be hopeful and give HIM a chance because your life really does depend on it.

1Corinthians 6:9-11 ~ [9] Or do you not know that the unrighteous will not inherit the kingdom of God? Do not be deceived; neither fornicators, nor idolaters, nor adulterers, nor effeminate, nor homosexuals, [10] nor thieves, nor *the* covetous, nor drunkards, nor revilers, nor swindlers, will inherit the kingdom of God. [11] Such were some of you; but you were washed, but you were sanctified, but you were justified in the name of the Lord Jesus Christ and in the Spirit of our God.

These words, which at first seem so threatening, shall become some of the sweetest words in the Bible as they are understood.

True, they mention homosexuality and being effeminate as two separate sins, but among all of the other sins that, if not repented of, bar people from the Kingdom of GOD.

They're not listed first, as if they are the worst of sins; nor do they mention them last as if they are unspeakable. They are listed in the middle, along with sins like greed and slander--no better, but yet no worse than the other sins.

Those words, "and such were some of you" tell us that some early Christians had struggled with homosexuality and had found Forgiveness and Freedom! Almighty YAHWEH is the same yesterday, today, and forever more (Hebrews 13:8).

Therefore, the ONE Who delivered them can also forgive and free us! We have solid Hope drawn from GOD'S Own Word!

At this time, please consider what you've read and learned, and journal your own personal response to this. This can be of great help in the future to see how you are progressing and changing.

4. What is one reason GOD gave commandments in the Bible?

Deuteronomy 6:24 ~ ²⁴ So the LORD commanded us to observe all these statutes, to fear the LORD our God for our good always and for our survival, as *it is* today.

GOD commands a course of duty, or right action, that we may learn to be Holy and stand firmly & righteously in HIS Love. HIS very law is a gift and a great benefit. Holiness is happiness, and that is our call, to be Holy.

Deuteronomy 10:12-13 ~ ¹² "Now, Israel, what does the LORD your God require from you, but to fear the LORD your God, to walk in all His ways and love Him, and to serve the LORD your God with all your heart and with all your soul, ¹³ *and* to keep the LORD's commandments and His statutes which I am commanding you today for your good?

The 'do's and don'ts' are there only to guide us toward a better, and holier life. Just like an owner's manual advises you not to put oil in your gas tank, the Bible instructs us to do certain things and refrain from doing others.

Just as you might be able to drive your car a while without an oil change, further down the road the damage caused by your neglect will reveal itself.

Look where you are now. Just as the car whose owner neglects to care for it will eventually fall apart, so will the person who neglects the wisdom in the Word of GOD.

Psalm 119:1 ~ How blessed are those whose way is blameless, Who walk in the law of the LORD.

"All men would be happy, but few take the right way; God has here laid before us the right way, which we may be sure will end in happiness, though it be straight and narrow. Blessings are to the righteous." ~ M. Henry

Proverbs 8:36 ~ 36 "But he who sins against me injures himself; All those who hate me love death.

To say a man might disobey and be none the worse would be to say that no might be yes and light sometimes darkness.

How many of us know that temporary relief can lead to misery? We've had to learn this. That may cause many to question GOD and/or HIS Will and Purpose. But we must remember that we chose to walk in the way we did.

I find encouragement in that fact because HE allowed me to endure all that I did for such a time as this! So be encouraged! You have been allowed to endure the life you have and trained up for a purpose! Now you have an assignment.

Jeremiah 32:39 ~ 39 and I will give them one heart and one way, that they may fear Me always, for their own good and for *the good of* their children after them.

"Well Jack", said one who met a man who had recently become a Christian, "I hear you have given up all your pleasures." "No, no" said Jack, "the fact lies the other way. I have just found all my pleasures, and I have only given up my follies." ~ C. H. Spurgeon

Matthew 6:33 ~ [33] But seek ye first the kingdom of God, and his righteousness; and all these things shall be added unto you.

Men can only be happy when they do not assume that the object of life is happiness. We are not called to happiness, but to holiness.

'Seek' carries the meaning of seeking earnestly, seeking intensely, living for it. And He enforces it by adding 'first'. That means principally, above everything else; give that priority. Many Christian people miss so many blessings...because they do not seek God diligently. ~ D. M. Lloyd-Jones

"Because of our addictions, we simply cannot--on our own--keep the great commandments. Most of us have tried, again and again, and failed. Some of us have even recognized that these commandments are really our own deepest desires. We have tried to dedicate our lives to them, but still we fail. I think our failure is necessary, for it is in failure and helplessness that we can most honestly and completely turn to grace. Grace is our only hope for dealing with addiction, the only power that can truly vanquish its destructiveness." ~ G. May

What many of us fail to realize is that we need more than just GOD'S Love to enter into HIS Kingdom. HE Loves us, oh yes, HE does. Each and every one of us! However, HIS Love doesn't get us into The Kingdom of Heaven. HIS Mercy does that!

Nothing can separate us from GOD'S Love, however, HIS Love will not get us into Heaven. We must obtain HIS Mercy in order to get into The Kingdom of Heaven.

Now while many don't even know that HIS Mercy is obtainable, I want us all to know that it is not only obtainable but retainable!

At this time, please consider what you've read and learned, and journal your own personal response to this. This can be of great help in the future to see how you are progressing and changing.

5. Where do temptations come from?

James 1:13-15 ~ [13] Let no one say when he is tempted, "I am being tempted by God"; for God cannot be tempted by evil, and He Himself does not tempt anyone. [14] But each one is tempted when he is carried away and enticed by his own lust. [15] Then when lust has conceived, it gives birth to sin; and when sin is accomplished, it brings forth death.

We must not blame GOD for our temptations, shaking our fists in HIS Face and screaming, "Why have you made me this way?" GOD has not made us this way! Remember, "born into sin but shaped in iniquity". Created in the image of GOD but born in the image of Adam. Created Holy and Righteous, but born sinful and perverse.

We must admit that the problem is our own. It comes from within us, possibly as a result of a failed relationship with one, or both, of our parents and possibly from some type of trauma in our lives or childhood.

Once we acknowledge this Truth, we can bring the resources of Grace to bear on our struggle and begin our journey to Freedom. Until then, we are doomed to remain stuck in our sin.

Michael Glatze, a former gay advocate, who was rescued by CHRIST, has written a lot of articles on this topic and one quote from his article I found to be very true is, "Homosexuality delivered to young minds, it is by its very nature, pornographic. It destroys impressionable minds and confuses their developing sexuality."

I know that to be true. Through being molested several times and then identifying that type of behavior with "love" is what began my downward spiral.

I know many of you can relate and/or identify with this, so I will make sure I tell you to be prepared to release every single thing that you have pent up, built up, stored away, hidden, denied and even forgotten because when HE washes you clean it will all come out, be exposed and will no longer hold any power over you, your thoughts, your feelings or your actions!

At this time, please consider what you've read and learned, and journal your own personal response to this. This can be of great help in the future to see how you are progressing and changing.

6. Can I overcome sexual brokenness by myself?

Jeremiah 13:23 ~ [23] "Can the Ethiopian change his skin or the leopard his spots? *Then* you also can do good who are accustomed to doing evil.

Almost all addiction programs begin with a very similar first step: I am powerless. As a Child of GOD that is similar to The Way, 'Nothing in my hand I bring, helpless I come to Thee for grace.'

If we think that we alone can do anything about our brokenness then we need a rude awakening and will probably get one if we haven't already.

C. H. Spurgeon once said that if GOD told people to crawl back and forth from here to Rome on their hands and knees they would want to do it; but the hardest advice to take is that there is nothing you can do.

Romans 5:6 ~ [6] For while we were still helpless, at the right time Christ died for the ungodly.

Usually the last thing we do is admit we are wrong, or that we are powerless against a vice or stronghold. But that should be the very first thing we do if we are going to move forward knowing that it is true.

At this time, please consider what you've read and learned, and journal your own personal response to this. This can be of great help in the future to see how you are progressing and changing.

7. Does being a Christian, or Follower of JESUS, enable me to overcome sexual brokenness by myself?

Romans 7:19 ~ [19] For the good that I want, I do not do, but I practice the very evil that I do not want.

"Lord," said Augustine, "deliver me from my worst enemy, that wicked man--myself."

A Leadership magazine survey revealed that twenty-three percent of the three hundred pastors who responded had done something sexually inappropriate with someone other than their spouse.

"Sin keeps house with us whether we will or not; the best saint alive is troubled with inmates; though he forsakes his sins, yet his sins will not forsake him." ~ Thomas Watson

If we know it, but allow it, then we are spitting in the face of our Creator. Whatever you know needs to change, be changed, stopped or removed, just do it!

Galatians 5:17 ~ [17] For the flesh sets its desire against the Spirit, and the Spirit against the flesh; for these are in opposition to one another, so that you may not do the things that you please.

At this time, please consider what you've read and learned, and journal your own personal response to this. This can be of great help in the future to see how you are progressing and changing.

8. What about my own intelligence and determination?

Admitting being powerless is a terrifying step, maybe even one we are resisting. To admit being powerless means that we have to acknowledge that all of our efforts at control are ineffective, but to abandon them seems like it may invite chaos and turmoil into our lives. The world tells us not to be weak, but that only the strong survive.

What would be left to us if we let go of all our elaborate systems of control? Who would control us if we could not control ourselves?

To admit powerlessness makes us feel like fools and failures, and some of us have spent many years trying to become strong to compensate for deep feelings of inferiority, low self-worth, codependency and/or inadequacy... and the list goes on.

To admit powerlessness means that we must trust others to help us, and many of us find tremendous difficulty trusting anyone because of our own unresolved hurt and/or pain.

To admit that we are powerless is to admit our need of The One True Living GOD, and many of us do not really want HIM in our lives. So, we continue our pointless and useless struggles.

Proverbs 3:5-6 ~ [5] Trust in the LORD with all your heart and do not lean on your own understanding. [6] In all your ways acknowledge Him, and He will make your paths straight.

"We do not have the ability in ourselves to accomplish the least of God's tasks. When we recognize it is impossible for us to perform a duty in our own strength, we will discover the secret of its accomplishment. But alas, this is a secret we often fail to discover." ~ J. Owen

Jeremiah 10:23 ~ [23] I know, O LORD, that a man's way is not in himself, nor is it in a man who walks to direct his steps.

Charlotte Eliza Kasl says, 'Addiction is, essentially, a spiritual breakdown, a journey away from the truth into emotional blindness and death.' As the thinking and the behavior of the addict moves further and further away from reality, thinking processes become impaired. Sexual addicts become progressively dishonest, self-centered, isolated, fearful, confused, devoid of feelings, dualistic, controlling, perfectionistic, blinded to their sin (denial), insane, blaming (projection), and dysfunctional. In short, their lives become progressively unmanageable.

We lie loudest when we lie to ourselves!

John 15:5 ~ [5] I am the vine, you are the branches; he who abides in Me and I in him, he bears much fruit, for apart from Me you can do nothing.

I am "a branch intimately and vitally joined to the vine"--not just tacked on to the vine, but actually a part of it. Just as the life of that vine flows naturally into the branch, so the life of Jesus The Christ flows naturally into me. But the analogies of the branch on the vine and the members of the body should not be pressed so far as to give the impression that we are passive in our union with Christ. Jesus told us to remain, or to abide, in Him.

"We must renounce all confidence in our own wisdom, power, and merit, instead looking entirely to Christ for what we need to live the Christian life. But what makes the looking to Him effective and fruitful is the fundamental fact that we are in Him. That is what God has done in calling us into fellowship with His Son, Jesus Christ.

He has brought us into a vital relationship with Christ that is as intimate as the relationship of the branch to the vine and the body to the head. He has made us to share in the very life of Christ Himself." ~ J. Bridges

At this time, please consider what you've read and learned, and journal your own personal response to this. This can be of great help in the future to see how you are progressing and changing.

9. Can I depend solely on the wisdom of men to gain Freedom from my unwanted sexual desires/lusts?

Do not go to a homosexual to find out if there is Freedom from homosexuality. Much the same a drug addict would not go ask a drug dealer if there is a way to get clean.

Psalm 1:1-3 ~ [1] How blessed is the man who does not walk in the counsel of the wicked, nor stand in the path of sinners, nor sit in the seat of scoffers! [2] But his delight is in the law of the LORD, And in His law [instructions] he meditates day and night. [3] He will be like a tree *firmly* planted by streams of water, which yields its fruit in its season and its leaf does not wither; and in whatever he does, he prospers.

Some of us were so very confused because we had chosen to listen to people in the sinful world, instead of listening to GOD.

The lies that we accept are part of the deception. We are indoctrinated through every which way. Between culture and society, there is no way anyone can get Truth, because those people do not even believe in Truth, they believe there is their truth and your truth.

I get it. For a while, all seems well with our choices, then the pain, which inevitably comes from walking in ways contrary to GOD'S Will, just overwhelms us. At first, shame keeps us from reaching out. Fortunately, the hurt gets so bad that we finally say, "I will arise and go to my FATHER."

Psalm 118:8 ~ It is better to take refuge in the LORD than to trust in man.

Proverbs 12:15 ~ The way of a fool is right in his own eyes, but a wise man is he who listens to counsel.

While there are people the Bible warns us not to listen to, there are others the Bible encourages us to heed. Many of us were too proud or too frightened to seek outside help, and so continued to suffer until, in desperation, we overcame our fears, we swallowed our pride, and reached out to those who could offer godly help.

Proverbs 15:22 ~ Without consultation, plans are frustrated, but with many counselors they succeed.

Some of us, passive by nature, were ready to swallow anything we were told without responsible evaluation. All men are limited, and even the wisest and best can err; and, as sinners, men distort or even deny the Truth. The Bible is GOD'S touchstone by which we must test the teachings of men.

And even when men teach the Truth, they cannot give us the strength to practice it. GOD'S HOLY SPIRIT must give us that Power if we are to live and walk in Truth. We should learn from others, but we must depend on The LORD GOD Almighty!

Acts 17:11 ~ Now these were more noble-minded than those in Thessalonica, for they received the word with great eagerness, examining the Scriptures daily *to see* whether these things were so.

In our present fallen condition, it is impossible to think out a standard of duty which shall be warped by none of our prejudices, distorted by none of our passions, and corrupted by none of our habits. It is only of the law of the Lord as contained in the Scriptures that we can justly say, "It is perfect."

1John 4:1 ~ Beloved, do not believe every spirit, but test the spirits to see whether they are from God, because many false prophets have gone out into the world.

"Everything in the railway service depends upon the accuracy of the signals. When these are wrong, life will be sacrificed. On the road to Heaven we need unerring signals, or the catastrophes will be far more terrible." ~ C. H. Spurgeon

At this time, please consider what you've read and learned, and journal your own personal response to this. This can be of great help in the future to see how you are progressing and changing.

10. Where can I turn for real help with sexual brokenness?

Isaiah 55:6 ~ Seek the LORD while He may be found; Call upon Him while He is near.

This verse tells us something very important, and matter of fact; that GOD'S patience is exhaustible. It says to seek HIM "while" HE may be found and call on HIM "while" HE is near. That tells me that there may be a time that HE will not be near and won't be found. The time of salvation is now! Right now!!

John 8:34 ~ Jesus answered them, "Truly, truly, I say to you, everyone who commits sin is the slave of sin.

One of the most encouraging and 'freeing' Truths I ever learned was that in order to be Free I needed to become a bond servant. Being a bond-servant to YAHWEH, GOD Almighty, *is Freedom*!

Remaining in sin, means remaining a slave. Big difference between a slave and a bond-servant. More on a bond-servant at the end of this section.

"The sinner thinks sin is his tool, but he himself is the tool of sin. Sin obtains the mastery of his affections and will, and when the galling chains are felt, and efforts made to break through them, the awful tyranny is realized." ~ G. Reith

"Servitude degrades people to such a point that they come to like it."

John 8:36 ~ So if the Son makes you free, you will be free indeed.

"To deliver men from this bondage is the grand object of the Gospel. To awaken people to a sense of their degradation, to show them their chains, to make them arise and struggle to be free, this is the great end for which Christ sent forth His ministers." ~ J. C. Ryle

The Son makes you free (John 8:36), so trust Him and follow Him. His truth makes you free (John 8:32), so study it, believe it, and obey it. Satan imposes slavery that seems like freedom (2 Peter 2:19); Jesus gives you a yoke that makes you free (Matthew 11:28-30).

Romans 8:2 ~ For the law of the Spirit of life in Christ Jesus has set you free from the law of sin and of death.

2 Corinthians 3:5 ~ Not that we are adequate in ourselves to consider anything as *coming* from ourselves, but our adequacy is from God

Addiction can be, and often is, the thing that brings us to our knees. Addiction teaches us not to be too proud, sooner or later, addiction will prove to us that we are not gods.

Because I have been on my deathbed and accepted my life was over, and that I would not survive, I can truly recognize the magnitude of the gift as well as the magnitude of my sin. This life is not my own. Every breath I have belongs to HIM and HIM Alone.

2 Corinthians 12:7-10 ~ [7] Because of the surpassing greatness of the revelations, for this reason, to keep me from exalting myself, there was given me a thorn in the flesh, a messenger of Satan to torment me — to keep me from exalting myself! [8] Concerning this I implored the Lord three times that it might leave me. [9] And He has said to me, "My grace is sufficient for you, for power is perfected in weakness." Most gladly, therefore, I will rather boast about my weaknesses, so that the power of Christ may dwell in me. [10] Therefore I am well content with weaknesses, with insults, with distresses, with persecutions, with difficulties, for Christ's sake; for when I am weak, then I am strong.

Discovering our true identity is an experience of being changed by a loving and supportive FATHER Who knows what we need and helps us through our pain to see and give up our selfish agendas and surrender to HIS Will.

At times we are excited and delighted witnesses to our transformation. At other times we are immersed in pain and discouragement at the slow pace of change, but with less and less fear of such pain & more and more confidence that we will emerge on the other side of it in a better place, closer to GOD.

These steps are most effective when taken in the context of:

1. Attending group meetings (and if group meetings are not possible, find someone that you can Trust to be open and honest with, someone you can communicate with in person or via email, snail-mail, Skype, etc., someone who you can be accountable to)

2. Praying and meditating on The Word of GOD daily. Study.

3. Accepting guidance from someone (brethren, minister) through the process of working these methods.

4. Giving away what you are finding. Sharing your Joy with others as you discover it.

At this time, please consider what you've read and learned, and journal your own personal response to this. This can be of great help in the future to see how you are progressing and changing.

Quick Lesson: Bond-servant vs Slave ~ When a slave was being set free but did not want to leave their master, their home, family, friends, etc.... then they would choose to be a "bond-servant" and they would then get their ear pierced with a piece of wood, done on the doorway, or door jam, to show and prove to everyone that they are no longer a slave but a bond-servant and there because they choose to be.

More Info: Bond-servant vs slave ~ There are two types of servitude referred to in the Bible. One describes a slave and the other is a "bond-slave" or "bondservant".

Why is the concept of a bondservant so significant for the Church today? There is a growing movement throughout the world encouraging people to stand up and demand their personal rights and freedoms.

Sadly, this thinking is also surfacing within the Body of CHRIST. The Word of GOD however, teaches us that when we accept JESUS The CHRIST as our Lord and Savior, we must be willing to give up these rights in favor of assuming a position as a willing servant to The CHRIST and to HIS Church.

This is a new and revolutionary attitude for some people living today, including most Christians. Even in JESUS' day, it was contrary to popular thinking. Nobody wants to become a slave, they wanted to be free from slavery. Not even knowing that anyone in sin is a slave to sin.

Paul describes the perspective JESUS had as a bondservant when HE suffered the indignities of The Cross:

Philippians 2:5-8 ~ [5] Have this attitude in yourselves which was also in Christ Jesus, [6] who, although He existed in the form of God, did not regard equality with God a thing to be grasped, [7] but emptied Himself, taking the form of a bond-servant, *and* being made in the likeness of men. [8] Being found in appearance as a man, He humbled Himself by becoming obedient to the point of death, even death on a cross.

YESHUA, JESUS The CHRIST, humbled HIMSELF as a slave would humble himself and became obedient to the point of death. HE did not protest his rough treatment, humiliation, the scourging, cruel whipping, or the beatings prior to being nailed to The Cross.

HE understood and accepted the fact that a bondservant had no personal rights. And HE needed to demonstrate for us, those who would follow in the way of The Cross, what accepting bondservanthood truly meant. It is a Glorious occasion!

This distinguishing characteristic of JESUS The CHRIST, as a bondservant, should also be the distinguishing trait of HIS Body, The Church. HE told the disciples on several occasions that to be great one must willingly take on the lifestyle of a bondservant.

Each major writer of the New Testament referred to himself as a bondservant. Peter, Paul, John (Revelation 1:1), James (James 1:1), and Jude (Jude 1) all described themselves in this manner; it further emphasized the burning desire within them to be identified with JESUS. And if you study the lives of these great men of GOD, you will discover that after they made the commitment to live their lives as bondservants, HE raised them up in the Body of CHRIST as leaders.

You see, "bondservant" in the Kingdom of GOD, is another way of saying "leader."

This is someone that people look up to and watch closely in order to pattern their lives after them. And this is particularly true for young people who eagerly launch into projects and events with great enthusiasm and passion but need the direction of godly leaders to build solid Truth into their lives. They need role models who carry the mark of a "bondservant" proudly and boldly.

Now we aren't going to pierce our ear with a piece of wood on a door jam, but the "mark" of our bond-servanthood is how we represent YESHUA, JESUS The CHRIST, in our Word, our Deed and our Action.

When we become these servants of The Most High GOD, then we will fit in well with the scene of the New Jerusalem described in the Book of Revelation:

"...and His bond-servants will serve Him; they will see His face, and His name will be on their foreheads."

Revelation 22:3b-4

Six of the most outstanding qualities that GOD builds into HIS bondservants are:

1. Diligence – A bondservant works from sun-up to sundown without complaint, knowing that The Master demands and requires a full day of labor.

2. Courage – Adversity will be faced and conquered in order to accomplish the task set before them by The Master.

3. Humility – Not a false humility that was symbolic of the Pharisees, but a true brokenness born out of a realistic understanding of our position before a loving and caring Master.

4. Dependence – A bondservant trusts The Master to provide all the needed supplies including food, clothes, and shelter.

5. Identity – Bondservants are not ashamed of being identified with their Master or HIS Family (The Church). They boldly confess JESUS The CHRIST as their LORD and their SAVIOR and proudly carry the Family Name.

6. Single-mindedness – The focus of a bondservant is on the priorities of The Master. JESUS' Will was The FATHER'S Will, and that must become the bondservant's will/desires.

"... let us also lay aside every encumbrance and the sin which so easily entangles us, and let us run with endurance the race that is set before us, fixing our eyes on Jesus, the author and perfecter of faith, who for the joy set before Him endured the cross, despising the shame, and has sat down at the right hand of the throne of God. For consider Him who has endured such hostility by sinners against Himself, so that you will not grow weary and lose heart."

Hebrews 12:1-3

11. Will I need the help of others as well?

Ecclesiastes 4:9-12 ~ [9] Two are better than one because they have a good return for their labor. [10] For if either of them falls, the one will lift up his companion. But woe to the one who falls when there is not another to lift him up. [11] Furthermore, if two lie down together they keep warm, but how can one be warm *alone*? [12] And if one can overpower him who is alone, two can resist him. A cord of three *strands* is not quickly torn apart.

"God has made no provision in the Bible for isolation. Scripture expressions all show a contrary state of things: We are 'branches' in the vine, 'members' in the body, 'stones' in the temple, 'brothers and sisters' in the family..." ~ D. L. Moody

1 Thessalonians 5:11 ~ Therefore encourage one another and build up one another, just as you also are doing.

RESIDUE is not a recovery program because once you've encountered YESHUA, JESUS The CHRIST, and have surrendered to HIM totally, you are recovered! This is not one of those programs that is going to lie to you and fill your head with a victim-mentality telling you that you have a "disease" and once an addict always an addict. That is a lie from the pit of hell!

Many say that GOD is their support group, or they go to HIM with their confessions. GOD'S Spirit is within each of those that have become HIS Children, so allow HIM to be your support group through HIS Spirit that dwelleth within HIS

Own. Find a support group!

We must desire to experience the reality of our GOD'S Love through relationships with HIS people, who also struggle with similar issues.

Healing and change occur through a network of brethren, a support group. And I don't mean attending an occasional meeting. I mean attending on a regular basis while also remaining in contact on an almost daily basis if possible.

This is scary, I know. But a lot of times a person will attend one group meeting, find something wrong with it, and use that as an excuse to forsake all group meetings. The individual finds it easier to see flaws in the support group than to work through the pain and flaws in his or her own life.

2Timothy 2:22 ~ [22] Now flee from youthful lusts and pursue righteousness, faith, love *and* peace, with those who call on the Lord from a pure heart.

At this time, please consider what you've read and learned, and journal your own personal response to this. This can be of great help in the future to see how you are progressing and changing.

12. What might keep me from getting the help I need?

Jeremiah 17:9 ~ The heart is deceitful above all things, and desperately wicked: who can know it?

Clancy runs a mission for skid-row alcoholics in Los Angeles. Tells stories of holding many of them in his arms as they die from their alcoholism. And as they die, they protest, 'It wasn't the booze'

Clancy then describes his own experience. "The use of booze and drugs was killing me. And even though I could rationally see that fact, I could not believe it because my gut told me that my survival depended on continuing to use the stuff. And the more dependent I became, the more I believed my gut."

John 9:40-41 ~ [40] Those of the Pharisees who were with Him heard these things and said to Him, "We are not blind too, are we?" [41] Jesus said to them, "If you were blind, you would have no sin; but since you say, 'We see,' your sin remains.

The healing of the blind man (in John 9) is presented as a parable of spiritual illumination. Thanks to the coming of the true light into the world, many who were formerly in darkness have been enlightened. But some who thought they had no need of the enlightenment He brought turned their backs on Him and, without realizing it, moved into deeper darkness. Had they acknowledged their spiritual blindness and allowed Him to remove it, they would have been blessed.

Had they lived in darkness and found no way out into the light, their plight would have been sad, but no blame would have attached to them. Blame did attach to those who, while living in darkness, claimed to be able to see. To be so self-deceived as to shut one's eyes to The Light is a desperate state to be in: The Light is there, but if people reject it, how can they be enlightened? As Jesus said, their sin remains." ~ F. F. Bruce

Hebrews 3:13 ~ But encourage one another day after day, as long as it is *still* called "Today," so that none of you will be hardened by the deceitfulness of sin.

"Many people have difficulty admitting that any part of their lives has become unmanageable. We tend to think--perhaps because we like to think--that we are in control of everything." ~ A. Twerski

The refusal to recognize that things have gotten out of control is called denial. Denial is not the same as lying, because in denial the person actually believes in his or her own distortion of reality. Here is a good rule of thumb: If something causes a problem, it is a problem. Making believe that it is not will only allow the problem to continue.

When reality tries to tell you something, listen!

1 John 1:8 ~ If we say that we have no sin, we are deceiving ourselves and the truth is not in us.

Did you ever watch babies put their hands over their eyes to hide from you? Infants think that when they cannot see you, you cannot see them.

Like other forms of infantile thinking, this sometimes persists into adult life. There are people who believe that when they are oblivious to something, it simply does not exist.

Revelation 3:17 ~ Because you say, "I am rich, and have become wealthy, and have need of nothing," and you do not know that you are wretched and miserable and poor and blind and naked

At this time, please consider what you've read and learned, and journal your own personal response to this. This can be of great help in the future to see how you are progressing and changing.

13. Might I have distorted ideas of GOD?

Since we tend to associate our Heavenly FATHER with our earthly father, the answer is, an easy yes. If our earthly father was mean, then we believe GOD to be mean also. If he was strict or abusive or not present, then we assume GOD is the same way.

Psalm 50:21 ~ "These things you have done and I kept silence; You thought that I was just like you; I will reprove you and state *the case* in order before your eyes.

Isaiah 40:28 ~ Do you not know? Have you not heard? The Everlasting God, the LORD, the Creator of the ends of the earth does not become weary or tired. His understanding is inscrutable.

John 16:1-3 ~ [1] "These things I have spoken to you so that you may be kept from stumbling. [2] They will make you outcasts from the synagogue, but an hour is coming for everyone who kills you to think that he is offering service to God. [3] These things they will do because they have not known the Father or Me.

1Corinthians 1:20-21 ~ [20] Where is the wise man? Where is the scribe? Where is the debater of this age? Has not God made foolish the wisdom of the world? [21] For since in the wisdom of God the world through its wisdom did not *come to* know God, God was well-pleased through the foolishness of the message preached to save those who believe.

At this time, please consider what you've read and learned, and journal your own personal response to this. This can be of great help in the future to see how you are progressing and changing.

14. How can I correct my distorted ideas of GOD?

John 1:18 ~ No one has seen God at any time; the only begotten God who is in the bosom of the Father, He has explained *Him*.

John 14:8-9 ~ [8] Philip said to Him, "Lord, show us the Father, and it is enough for us." [9] Jesus said to him, "Have I been so long with you, and *yet* you have not come to know Me, Philip? He who has seen Me has seen the Father; how *can* you say, 'Show us the Father'?

Hebrews 1:1-3 ~ God, after He spoke long ago to the fathers in the prophets in many portions and in many ways, [2] in these last days has spoken to us in His Son, whom He appointed heir of all things, through whom also He made the world. [3] And He is the radiance of His glory and the exact representation of His nature, and upholds all things by the word of His power. When He had made purification of sins, He sat down at the right hand of the Majesty on high

GOD has perfectly revealed HIMSELF to man in JESUS The CHRIST. As we behold HIM in the Bible, the HOLY SPIRIT gradually replaces our false ideas of GOD with Truth. As the Truth passes from our conscious into our unconscious, healing takes place in our relationship with The FATHER. What a beautiful moment that is!

At this time, please consider what you've read and learned, and journal your own personal response to this. This can be of great help in the future to see how you are progressing and changing.

15. Can I approach GOD when I have doubts?

Mark 9:24 ~ Immediately the boy's father cried out and said, "I do believe; help my unbelief."

We readily confess that our faith is weak and timid at times. We struggle with periods of doubt. Do we forfeit God's blessing because we are weak in faith? Consider Abraham, the father of believers. His faith was not always unfailing and strong. He had his moments of doubt and despair. Yet God blessed him. When the father of the epileptic said to Jesus, 'I do believe, help me overcome my unbelief!' Jesus heard his prayer. He healed the man's son. Note, however, that this man struggled with his weak faith and asked for help. He received it.

Luke 17:5-6 ~ [5] The apostles said to the Lord, "Increase our faith!" [6] And the Lord said, "If you had faith like a mustard seed, you would say to this mulberry tree, 'Be uprooted and be planted in the sea'; and it would obey you.

"Their view of faith was certainly very wrong. They saw it as a kind of power with differing degrees of intensity. But the power of faith is not contained in faith itself but in God, whom we know by faith. Therefore, Jesus answered that if they had faith as small as a mustard seed, they would be able to order a mulberry tree to be uprooted and it would be done. God, in whom they put their trust, would work the impossible." ~ S. G. De Graff

John 7:17 ~ If anyone is willing to do His will, he will know of the teaching, whether it is of God or *whether* I speak from Myself.

Dr. R. A. Torrey wrote, "I have found no passage in the Bible equal to John 7:17 in dealing with an honest skeptic." Our GOD is so Good that HE not only Blesses those with weak Faith, but reaches out to those with no Faith, if they are willing. Our first attempt at obedience can only come after we have gained some measure of Faith, and The LORD our GOD becomes not just some blurred or obscure force, but very real and present to us. Our idea of who HE is changes as we realize HE is What HE said HE is in HIS Word!

He points to the depths of our identity, as intended, that we are not in touch with. We discover we do not know ourselves very well. HE reveals to each of us the identity crisis and the cure.

Romans 10:17 ~ So faith *comes* from hearing, and hearing by the word of Christ.

"I prayed for faith and thought that someday faith would come down and strike me like lightening. But faith did not seem to come. One day I read in the tenth chapter of Romans, 'Now faith comes by hearing, and hearing by the Word of God.' I had closed my Bible and prayed for faith. I now opened my Bible and began to study, and faith has been growing ever since." ~ D. L. Moody

At this time, please consider what you've read and learned, and journal your own personal response to this. This can be of great help in the future to see how you are progressing and changing.

16. Does GOD Love me?

Jeremiah 31:3 ~ The LORD appeared to him from afar, *saying*, "I have loved you with an everlasting love; Therefore I have drawn you with lovingkindness.

I am convinced that the simple affirmation 'GOD is Love' really is the answer to everything as long as we use it in context. GOD is Love, but HE is also Judgement and Wrath, this we can understand only after conviction and progression in HIS Truth.

Imagine if we can live the truth that HE is Love, and not just recite it or print it on wall hangings. Imagine that if we did this, we just might find both the power to combat evil and a place of rest in the midst of our struggles.

While many understand that GOD is Love, they're not being taught that HIS Love is not what will get them into The Kingdom of Heaven. Only HIS Mercy can do that. We need to make sure everyone understands this.

When I lived as a transgender/homosexual prostitute I would have been able to tell you that "GOD Loves me!" But I never understood that HIS Love was not what I needed to obtain and that even with HIS Love I could still go to hell.

The need is great. People must understand that they do not need to obtain GOD'S Love, but HIS Grace and Mercy!

John 3:16-17 ~ [16] "For God so loved the world, that He gave His only begotten Son, that whoever believes in Him shall not perish, but have eternal life. [17] For God did not send the Son into the world to judge the world, but that the world might be saved through Him.

Who delivered up JESUS to die?

Not Judas, for money; not Pilate, for fear; not even the Jews for envy; but The FATHER, for Love!

Romans 5:8 ~ But God demonstrates His own love toward us, in that while we were yet sinners, Christ died for us.

God's love, expressed through His people, and woven into our lives by His Spirit and His Word can, over a period of time, bring healing even to our deepest wounds." ~ R. McGee

Ephesians 2:4-5 ~ [4] But God, being rich in mercy, because of His great love with which He loved us, [5] even when we were dead in our transgressions, made us alive together with Christ (by grace you have been saved)

I am convinced that the basic cause of some of the most disturbing emotional/spiritual problems which trouble evangelical Christians is the failure to receive and live out God's unconditional grace, and the corresponding failure to offer that grace to others.

1 John 4:9-10 ~ [9] By this the love of God was manifested in us, that God has sent His only begotten Son into the world so that we might live through Him. [10] In this is love, not that we loved God, but that He loved us and sent His Son *to be* the propitiation for our sins.

The room in which you study is full of radio frequencies. Though stations all around beam them at you constantly, you cannot hear them unless you have your radio on.

GOD too is beaming HIS Love to you, but for the message to get through, there must be a receiver. If you have wondered whether GOD Loves you, consider these words of CHRIST.

Revelation 3:20 ~ Behold, I stand at the door and knock; if anyone hears My voice and opens the door, I will come in to him and will dine with him, and he with Me.

At this time, please consider what you've read and learned, and journal your own personal response to this. This can be of great help in the future to see how you are progressing and changing.

17. Will GOD forgive and accept me?

Psalm 130:3-4 ~ [3] If You, LORD, should mark iniquities, O Lord, who could stand? [4] But there is forgiveness with You, that You may be feared.

John 1:12 ~ [12] But as many as received Him, to them He gave the right to become children of God, *even* to those who believe in His name

JESUS came to die for the unrighteous, the inconsiderate, the thief, the adulterer, the pedophile, the selfish, the abuser, and for you.

As we grow in our understanding of HIS Love and continue to grasp the idea that HE can rescue anyone from the depths of their own darkness and deception. HE can rescue us from the condemnation we deserve, and when we understand that, then we will gradually become more patient and kind to others when they fail.

Isaiah 43:25 ~ "I, even I, am the one who wipes out your transgressions for My own sake, and I will not remember your sins.

Debbie Dortzbach, a missionary to Ethiopia, was held in captivity by some of those she came to serve. During that time she wrote: "Thank You God that though I have only dirty water to wash in You have reminded me as I look at the earth below me that my heart is washed pure white as this glistening marble rock beneath my feet. I am clean in the Righteousness of Jesus!"

Isaiah 53:5-6 ~ [5] But He was pierced through for our transgressions, He was crushed for our iniquities; The chastening for our well-being *fell* upon Him, and by His scourging we are healed. [6] All of us like sheep have gone astray, each of us has turned to his own way; But the LORD has caused the iniquity of us all to fall on Him.

"I often use a simple illustration in making the meaning of the verse plain. I let my right hand represent the inquirer, my left hand represents Christ, and my Bible represent the inquirer's sin. I first lay the Bible on my right hand and say, 'Now where is your sin?' The inquirer replies of course, 'On me.' I then repeat the last half of the verse, 'the Lord hath laid on Him the iniquity of us all,' and transfer the Bible from my right hand to my left, and ask, 'Where is your sin now?' The inquirer replies, 'On Him, of course.' I then ask, 'Is it on you any longer?' and he says, 'No, on Christ.'" ~ R. A. Torrey

Micah 7:18-19 ~ [18] Who is a God like You, who pardons iniquity and passes over the rebellious act of the remnant of His possession? He does not retain His anger forever, because He delights in unchanging love. [19] He will again have compassion on us; He will tread our iniquities under foot. Yes, You will cast all their sins into the depths of the sea.

"It is mercy to feed us, rich mercy to pardon us." ~ Thomas Watson

"Where God removes the guilt, he breaks the power of sin. With pardoning love God gives subduing grace." ~ Thomas Watson

Matthew 26:28 ~ for this is My blood of the covenant, which is poured out for many for forgiveness of sins.

"It is a folly to think that an emperor's revenue will not pay a beggar's debt. We have many sins, but God hath many mercies." ~ Thomas Manton IV

Luke 23:33-34 ~ [33] When they came to the place called The Skull, there they crucified Him and the criminals, one on the right and the other on the left. [34] But Jesus was saying, "Father, forgive them; for they do not know what they are doing." And they cast lots, dividing up His garments among themselves.

"His own racking agony did not make Him forget others. The first of His seven sayings on the cross was a prayer for the souls of His murderers. Let us see in our Lord's intercession for those who crucified Him, one more proof of Christ's infinite love to sinners. None are too wicked for Him to care for. None are too far gone in sin for His almighty heart to take interest about their souls. He wept over unbelieving Jerusalem. He heard the prayer of the dying thief. He stopped under the tree to call the publican Zacchaeus. He came down from Heaven to turn the heart of the persecutor Saul. Love like this is a love that passeth knowledge. The vilest of sinners have no cause to be afraid of applying to a Savior like this." ~ J. C. Ryle

Hebrews 8:12 ~ "FOR I WILL BE MERCIFUL TO THEIR INIQUITIES, AND I WILL REMEMBER THEIR SINS NO MORE."

The Compassion of JESUS inclines HIM to save sinners.

The Power of JESUS enables HIM to save sinners.

The Promises of JESUS bind HIM to save sinners.

John 6:37 ~ All that the Father gives Me will come to Me, and the one who comes to Me I will certainly not cast out.

Romans 3:24-26 ~ [24] being justified as a gift by His grace through the redemption which is in Christ Jesus; [25] whom God displayed publicly as a propitiation in His blood through faith. *This was* to demonstrate His righteousness, because in the forbearance of God He passed over the sins previously committed; [26] for the demonstration, *I say*, of His righteousness at the present time, so that He would be just and the justifier of the one who has faith in Jesus.

Romans 3:24-26 has been called "possibly the most important single paragraph ever written"

If some of the terms are unfamiliar to you, the following definitions will help.

JUSTIFIED: "The biblical meaning of 'justify' is to pronounce, accept, and treat as just. Paul proclaims the present justification of sinners by grace through faith in Jesus Christ, apart from works and despite demerit (Romans 3:21). The law has not been altered, or suspended for their justification, but fulfilled--by Jesus The Christ acting in their name. By perfectly serving God, Christ perfectly kept the law (Matthew 3:15). His obedience culminated in death (Philippians 2:8); He bore the penalty of the law in men's place (Galatians 3:13), to make propitiation for their sins (Romans 3:25). On the ground of Christ's obedience, God does not impute sin, but imputes righteousness, to sinners who believe, repent and are baptized (Romans 4:2-8; 5:19)." ~ J. I. Packer

GRACE: "God's spontaneous, unmerited favor in action, His freely bestowed lovingkindness in operation, bestowing the hope of eternal salvation upon guilt-laden sinners who turn to Him for refuge. Think of the Judge who not only remits the penalty but also cancels the guilt of the offender and even adopts him as His own child." ~ W. Hendriksen

REDEMPTION: "Has its origin in the release of prisoners of war on payment of a price (the 'ransom'). It was extended to include the freeing of slaves, again by the payment of a price. Among the Hebrews it could be used for release of a prisoner under sentence of death (Exodus 21:29-30), once more by the payment of a price." ~ L. Morris

PROPITIATION: Or "reconciling sacrifice" or "expiation or atonement" "means that Christ has satisfied the holy wrath of God through His payment for sin. There was only one reason for Him to do this: He loves us; infinitely, eternally, unconditionally and irrevocably." ~ R. McGee

"He hung upon the cross that we might sit upon the throne. His crucifixion is our coronation." ~ Thomas Watson

To sense the power which comes from taking the Truth of this section unto yourself, consider this letter:

"Dear David: For so long as I have thought God was so against me. Like I was doomed before I began. Now it's like God is right there in the mud with me, helping me, and saying, 'No matter what happens, Me and you are going through this together and I'm not ever going to leave you.' I don't know what to say. I can't believe Jesus is really setting me free! Wow! Thank you for being the one He chose to lead my path. I love you. And better yet, I love God!

At this time, please consider what you've read and learned, and journal your own personal response to this. This can be of great help in the future to see how you are progressing and changing

18. Will GOD Love, Forgive, and accept me in spite of all that I am and all that I have done?

Isaiah 1:18 ~ "Come now, and let us reason together," says the LORD, "Though your sins are as scarlet, they will be as white as snow; Though they are red like crimson, they will be like wool.

"The greatest sinners, if they truly repent, shall have their sins forgiven. Though our sins have been as scarlet and crimson, a deep dye, a double dye, first in the wool of original corruption and afterwards in the many threads of actual transgression--though we have been often dipped, by our many backslidings, into sin, and though we have lain long soaking in it, yet pardoning mercy will thoroughly discharge the stain, and we shall be clean." ~ M. Henry

"If Christ had declined to associate with sinners, He would have had a lonely time on earth." ~ D. L. Moody

YAHWEH, GOD Almighty, having Created us, has a right to expect that we will love HIM above all. But have we not often ignored and even defied HIM? And yet HE Loves us still with an incredible Love!

Because of our rebellion, we deserve judgment and wrath. Instead, GOD Loves us so much that HE robed HIMSELF in flesh, becoming The Man JESUS The CHRIST, to live a sinless life in our place and die on the Cross for our sins. In CHRIST JESUS, a Holy GOD can fully accept us with all of our failures and weaknesses.

JESUS The CHRIST rose from the dead. If you have never asked HIM into your life, HE stands at the door of your heart seeking admittance. HE says, "I love you and long that we may be close. I want to forgive your sins. I'm ready to stand with you in all the struggles of life and will help you become all that The FATHER intends you to be. Come, share with ME forever."

At this time, please consider what you've read and learned, and journal your own personal response to this. This can be of great help in the future to see how you are progressing and changing

19. Since GOD Loves me, need I worry or fear?

Psalm 23:4 ~ Even though I walk through the valley of the shadow of death, I fear no evil, for You are with me; Your rod and Your staff, they comfort me.

Many of us used drugs, alcohol, violence, or sexual activity to deaden emotional pain. When life's difficulties seemed too much for us, we sought to lessen our pain by means of escape.

As we break this pattern, we may begin to have strong, uncomfortable, even frightening feelings as our emotional numbness wears off. We must resist the temptation to draw back and instead reach out to GOD and to HIS people, our brethren, to help us through our difficult periods.

Psalm 50:15 ~ Call upon Me in the day of trouble; I shall rescue you, and you will honor Me.

"We can only conquer doubts by looking steadily to Him and by not looking at them." ~ D. M. Lloyd-Jones

Psalm 55:22 ~ Cast your burden upon the LORD and He will sustain you; He will never allow the righteous to be shaken.

"We are safer with Him in the dark than without Him in the sunshine." ~ T. L. Cuyler

"He never promises us smooth paths, but He does promise safe ones." ~ ~ T. L. Cuyler

Matthew 6:34 ~ So do not worry about tomorrow; for tomorrow will care for itself. Each day has enough trouble of its own.

When we are feeling emotional pain or undergoing strong temptation, we may begin to wonder how we can go on for the rest of our lives without 'acting out'. Discouragement and depression can lead to defeat. At such times we need to remind ourselves that JESUS The CHRIST taught us to live "one day at a time." To get through life's troubles we must focus on the present--the moment at hand, the day in progress--leaving tomorrow's struggles for tomorrow.

Philippians 1:27 ~ Only conduct yourselves in a manner worthy of the gospel of Christ, so that whether I come and see you or remain absent, I will hear of you that you are standing firm in one spirit, with one mind striving together for the faith of the gospel

We would question the sanity of the greatest football player in history if he ever tried to play alone against the poorest of teams. Yet we often withdraw from others who are willing to help and isolate ourselves when we are having trouble.

GOD never intended for us to fight our battles alone. HE teaches us to reach out to HIM and to HIS people, our brethren, for help. We must not struggle alone but strive "together for the faith of the gospel".

Philippians 4:6-7 ~ [6] Be anxious for nothing, but in everything by prayer and supplication with thanksgiving let your requests be made known to God. [7] And the peace of God, which passes all comprehension, will guard your hearts and your minds in Christ Jesus.

At this time, please consider what you've read and learned, and journal your own personal response to this. This can be of great help in the future to see how you are progressing and changing

20. Will GOD be with me when I am tried and tempted?

These happen to be my favorite "go-to" verses:

James 1:2-3 ~ [2] Consider it all joy, my brethren, when you encounter various trials, [3] knowing that the testing of your faith produces endurance.

1 Corinthians 10:13 ~ No temptation has overtaken you but such as is common to man; and God is faithful, who will not allow you to be tempted beyond what you are able, but with the temptation will provide the way of escape also, so that you will be able to endure it.

Psalm 27:14 ~ Wait for the LORD; Be strong and let your heart take courage; Yes, wait for the LORD.

Dr. E. Wilson writes, "I firmly believe that deliverance from sexual obsession cannot take place apart from God. I am not, however, suggesting that God is a pill which can be taken as a magical cure. Deliverance is closely coupled with obedience and a willingness to make hard choices which may have to be made over and over again until the old behavior patterns are replaced by new sane habits. In this we all need God's enablement. He wants our cooperation."

Isaiah 41:10 ~ 'Do not fear, for I am with you; Do not anxiously look about you, for I am your God. I will strengthen you, surely I will help you, surely I will uphold you with My righteous right hand.'

Matthew 26:41 ~ Keep watching and praying that you may not enter into temptation; the spirit is willing, but the flesh is weak.

Trusting GOD does not mean that we have no responsibility for our own well-being. If we are to walk in The Way, then we must participate in our healing and in maintaining good emotional & spiritual health. As the old saying goes, "He who would eat the fruit must first climb the tree."

Romans 13:14 ~ But put on the Lord Jesus Christ and make no provision for the flesh in regard to *its* lusts.

If we want to stand, we must avoid situations which can lead to a fall. I heard a very wise saying: "If you don't want to slip, stay away from slippery places and slippery people."

When we have no choice, we need to prepare in advance for the battle. Our greatest safeguard against temptation is prayer. It is also good to tell a brother or sister of our danger and ask him or her to check with us periodically to see if we are having trouble. Remember, "If you fail to plan, you're planning to fail."

We need accountability.

There is no trap so deadly as the trap you set for yourself.

We can only stand firm as long as we remember our helplessness and our HELPER. When we become self-satisfied and/or self-confident rather than watchful and GOD-Confident, we are ripe, ready, and begging for a fall.

Psalm 37:23-24 ~ [23] The steps of a man are established by the LORD, and He delights in his way. [24] When he falls, he will not be hurled headlong, because the LORD is the One who holds his hand.

We all have different struggles and mature on different schedules. Some of us are acting out (engaging in the very thing we seek freedom from). All of us have problems with thoughts and deception. Some of us are out of control. Others gain and lose command of themselves several times as they work towards Freedom. Healing may be sudden or gradual. We are all unique.

Ephesians 2:1-9 ~ [1] And you were dead in your trespasses and sins, [2] in which you formerly walked according to the course of this world, according to the prince of the power of the air, of the spirit that is now working in the sons of disobedience. [3] Among them we too all formerly lived in the lusts of our flesh, indulging the desires of the flesh and of the mind, and were by nature children of wrath, even as the rest. [4] But God, being rich in mercy, because of His great love with which He loved us, [5] even when we were dead in our transgressions, made us alive together with Christ (by grace you have been saved), [6] and raised us up with Him, and seated us with Him in the heavenly *places* in Christ Jesus, [7] so that in the ages to come He might show the surpassing riches of His grace in kindness toward us in Christ Jesus. [8] For by grace you have been saved through faith; and that not of yourselves, *it is* the gift of God; [9] not as a result of works, so that no one may boast.

Moses was a murderer, "but GOD" forgave him and used him to deliver Israel from Egypt.

David was an adulterer and a murderer, "but GOD" forgave him and made him a great king.

Peter denied The LORD, "but GOD" forgave him, and Peter became a leader in the Church.

GOD rejoices when HIS children learn to accept HIS forgiveness, pick themselves up, and walk after they have stumbled.

Proverbs 28:13 -- He who conceals his transgressions will not prosper, but he who confesses and forsakes *them* will find compassion.

We must be patient with ourselves and each other and trust GOD to heal us in the way best for each one of us as individuals. In all our struggle, we must not allow guilt, shame, pain, confusion, or despair to overwhelm and isolate us from GOD or others. If we turn to GOD, HE will forgive us. HE will not abandon us but will stand with us in all our battles till freedom is ours!

At this time, please consider what you've read and learned, and journal your own personal response to this. This can be of great help in the future to see how you are progressing and changing

21. How does one react when experiencing GOD'S Love?

Psalm 40:1-3 ~ [1] I waited patiently for the LORD; And He inclined to me and heard my cry. [2] He brought me up out of the pit of destruction, out of the miry clay, and He set my feet upon a rock making my footsteps firm. [3] He put a new song in my mouth, a song of praise to our God; Many will see and fear and will trust in the LORD.

"Till you know the depth of the pit into which you have fallen, you will never properly Praise the hand which raises you out of it." ~ D. L. Moody

"In prayer we act like men; in praise we act like angels." ~ Thomas Watson

At this time, please consider what you've read and learned, and journal your own personal response to this. This can be of great help in the future to see how you are progressing and changing

Even as I began to study, and to walk in The Way it was difficult for me to believe that GOD accepted me when my conscience condemned me. I felt that the Scriptures which spoke of judgment all applied to me, and that those which spoke of Mercy were for others.

My experiences in life had taught me that people only love you as long as you please them. I couldn't stop thinking, from time to time, did GOD Love me in spite of it all? In spite of me being so malicious? Even in spite of me trying to purposely infect others with HIV/AIDS?

Seeing family, friends and even strangers turn away from me due to my sins, past behaviors and activities made it difficult to believe that GOD'S arms were open to receive me so easily.

Is it worth all the work? It sure is!

I claim the Truth, to anyone I come into contact with, that JESUS The CHRIST is the absolute only place where we can find Freedom. Freedom in any and every circumstance. Peace and Joy drive away the old depressions which were so crippling.

What can I render to GOD for going to such lengths to save me and call me HIS Own?

1) In your journal, write out as many examples of powerlessness and emotional unmanageability as a result of your struggles as you can remember. Discuss your findings.

2) Then write out as many examples as you can recall of your tendency to doubt the motives of people (especially your parents) when they were thoughtful and kind to you. Then write examples of whining, complaining, and detachment from GOD which reveal your doubt of HIS Love and acceptance. Discuss what you have found.

3) List something you can do this week to reach out in a new way to JESUS The CHRIST and to another human being. Share your decision.

3) Memorize one of the verses you found helpful in this section.

4) Read aloud Psalm 23 every morning when you awake and every evening before you go to sleep, praising GOD for the Truth of HIS Love extended to you despite your shortcomings and failures.

Psalm 23 ~ [1] The LORD is my shepherd, I shall not want.

[2] He makes me lie down in green pastures; He leads me beside quiet waters.

[3] He restores my soul; He guides me in the paths of righteousness for His name's sake.

[4] Even though I walk through the valley of the shadow of death, I fear no evil, for You are with me; Your rod and Your staff, they comfort me.

[5] You prepare a table before me in the presence of my enemies; You have anointed my head with oil; My cup overflows.

[6] Surely goodness and lovingkindness will follow me all the days of my life, and I will dwell in the house of The LORD forever.

I was always afraid to admit that I was powerless over my strongholds because I thought that to do so would mean the struggle was hopeless. If I could not bring my same-sex desires under control, I felt I was doomed to its being forever out of control.

I accepted that my thoughts and feelings were my identity. Once I put on the homosexual/transgender identity that is what dictated my friends, my relatives I'd associate with, where I lived, hung out, and the businesses I would patronize.

This identity decided my thoughts, feelings, emotional outbursts and how offended I was and when. This identity became every fiber of my being, of my world.

I expected GOD to deliver me all at once. HE heals in HIS time. This is not to torment, but to teach, to enable us to learn lessons about how HE works.

I expected GOD to deliver me without anyone else--just the two of us. HE delivers us through HIS Word and through HIS People.

To admit being powerless is not, of course, a once-and-for-all act. It is a daily decision to reach out to HIM through prayer and to others when lonely, frightened, stressed, hurting, in need. When GOD'S Will, becomes our will, we find Strength.

We are called to be a Living Sacrifice; to deny self, daily; to die, daily; to lift our Cross, daily! This is a daily process of sanctification that sets us apart as we learn and grow.

When I forget, and draw back, doing things in my old way, I stumble. No one should expect this life to be easy. Everyone faces problems which sometimes over-whelm, but you need not face your struggles alone. GOD Almighty and HIS Children are here for you.

Purpose of this lesson: To prepare ourselves to release the power our deepest and darkest secrets & sins hold over us. To know & Believe we are Forgiven regardless of all that we have done and had or have become.

We admit our helplessness. We confess that the lusts of our flesh and the strongholds of this world are more than we can handle alone. We do this to see our Hope. To learn of a loving and forgiving FATHER who will meet our unmet needs which have only fueled our struggle. To learn of, experience and gain Faith.

We do this to know and believe that we are forgiven. We will not instantly understand, but we will know it and believe it, implying that Faith does not come easily for many of us. Why is belief so difficult for some?

Our first and most influential ideas about GOD come from our early relationship with our parents. Unfortunately, many of us did not get on too well with our folks and so formed a mental image of GOD as someone who does not really care, who is distant, demanding, always disapproving, harsh, angry, cold, indifferent, rejecting, non-existent, etc.

We have given into one of the many deceptions the enemy has established; little girls are closer to daddy and little boys are closest to mommy. This has caused mothers to push their little girls more towards daddy and fathers have accepted the lie that their little boys will be closest to mommy. Breaking the natural GOD-Given plan of Intimacy with our same-sex parent.

Other ideas of GOD are sometimes caused, for some, by unhappy experiences with people within "the church" who they thought correctly represented GOD. Maybe they shared their struggle with a "Christian" who turned away from them or used that confession against them at some point. And so, they concluded (wrongly) that GOD must also be the same way.

Some were angry with GOD. Asking HIM repeatedly for help with the struggle, but nothing happened. Why was HE so silent? Had HE walked out on us? Did HE even care? Why did HE leave us to struggle alone? Why had HE not helped? These angry questions, and many more, raised disturbing doubts in our minds and drove many to not only question GOD'S Love, but to deny HIS very existence.

Many of us really hated ourselves because of what we had been doing and thinking. The guilt and shame we felt had deluded us into thinking that GOD must hate us at least as much as we despised ourselves. So, for many of us, thoughts of GOD were most unwelcome, bringing only feelings of fear and condemnation.

If you find thoughts of GOD difficult, please remember, "The only requirement for Freedom is a desire to be free." The struggle with being free will be more difficult in some ways than any of you have experienced before. You will have to deal, not only with outward actions or even inner thoughts, but with feelings that live at the very core of your existence and habits of a lifetime of being molded into the image the enemy had planned for you.

In this struggle to be Free, we have to find out who we are. We cannot trust our thoughts or feelings because our past has distorted them. We cannot trust friends, or associates, who share our delusions. Who can we trust? Who will gently show us who we are? Only JESUS The CHRIST can do that, and the process will continue through HIS Disciples.

I have learned this from my own experience and, if you continue, you will see HIM at work in your own life.

All this may be frightening to you. Just remember, you are loved for your courage in entering into the process of discovering your true identity in YESHUA, JESUS The CHRIST, and in confronting & dealing with the struggle of it.

Bear with us. Keep open and honest. Dare to experiment. Try to have an open mind. Work these methods & answer the questions you are ready for, leaving the others for later.

If you cannot work on your relationship with GOD now, work on your relationship with others. GOD is wonderfully patient. Do your best. Easy does it! One day at a time!

Method 2. See the purpose in our suffering and our failures. Learn from it.

Purpose 2. To know that we have been deceived, a deception that trapped us in a false identity.

So far we have faced our own powerlessness, and saw that "power belongeth unto GOD" (Psalm 62:11) Who "giveth power to them that have no might" (Isaiah 40:29); and, as we came to believe in HIS Love and Grace, we found "Joy and Peace in believing" (Romans 15:13).

Now, our newfound, or newly revived, Faith in the Love of GOD Almighty enables us to begin the attack at the very root of our strongholds, our struggles, our vice, our sin. Many of us felt like, and believed, that we were victims of life, victims of parents, victims of molesters, abusers and so on. And it may even be true! But if we stop there and see no thread of grace running through our sufferings, we end up being victims who have no Hope. Victim mentality runs deep, it is instilled in us from an incredibly young age on up, and this is not purposely, but because our focus has been distorted.

Whatever may have happened when we were young, we are children no longer and we must accept responsibility for our current actions, and for our actions from this point on. With GOD'S help, we can change. But as long as we blame others or circumstances over which we have no control, we will feel trapped, unable to do anything to change our lives. Bitterness and suspicion will lead us to develop an ever more distrustful attitude toward others and we will put up walls to keep them far away emotionally so that they cannot hurt us.

Loneliness is only one of the emotions, or feelings, that will drive us to acting out, which is only a feeble substitute for what we truly need, but from which we have cut ourselves off. Resentment may even poison our relationship with GOD as we angrily or pitifully ask, "Why me?"

If we are to find Freedom, we must undermine our feelings of being a victim and of self-pity. And to do so we must see YAHWEH, GOD Almighty, not only as our Loving FATHER, but also as our Sovereign LORD whose Awesome Grace can bring Blessing out of all that we have endured.

While we are not to blame for how this 'victim-mentality' has been brought upon the nations, we are responsible for the actions we take once we are schooled and informed of what has been happening for a few thousand years.

At this point, we have two choices; recognize or deny. As we grow up, we learn how easy it is to get attention and receive some pity or coddling; all we have to do is fall down, scrape an elbow, have an ache or pain, be sad, act depressed, and the list goes on and on and on!

This victim-mentality has been growing more than ever in the last 50 years or so and will continue to spread until the end. However, it no longer has to be an issue with you, or in your life because you have been awoken and are no longer in a deep slumber of ignorance and regret.

1. Since sin has come into the world, is life difficult for everyone?

Genesis 3:17-19 ~ [17] Then to Adam He said, "Because you have listened to the voice of your wife, and have eaten from the tree about which I commanded you, saying, 'You shall not eat from it'; Cursed is the ground because of you; In toil you will eat of it all the days of your life.

[18] "Both thorns and thistles it shall grow for you; And you will eat the plants of the field; [19] By the sweat of your face you will eat bread, till you return to the ground, because from it you were taken; For you are dust, and to dust you shall return."

Sin always brings sorrow. It has been so from the beginning.

"The whole earth partakes of the punishment, which the sin of man, its head and destined ruler, has called down. Death reigns. Instead of the blessed soil of Paradise, Adam and his offspring have to till the ground now condemned to bear thorns and thistles, and this is not to end, until man returns to the earth from which he was taken." ~ E. H. Browne

Job 14:1 ~ Man, who is born of woman, is short-lived and full of turmoil.

Everybody out there is hurting. And if you don't know that, you're either very naive and believe in the facades people put on, or so thick-skinned that you don't care, or hurt yourself, and don't feel other people's hurts either.

Someone once said that living is like licking honey off a cactus.

Ecclesiastes 1:2 ~ "Vanity of vanities," says the Preacher, "Vanity of vanities! All is vanity."

When Ernie Pyle, famed World War II correspondent, learned of the death of his mother, he wrote these touching words: "It seems to me that life is futile and death the final indignity. People live and suffer and grow bent with yearning, bowed with disappointment, and then they die. And what is it all for? I do not know."

Ecclesiastes 2:22-23 ~ [22] For what does a man get in all his labor and in his striving with which he labors under the sun? [23] Because all his days his task is painful and grievous; even at night his mind does not rest. This too is vanity.

Life is not just a struggle for you; it's a struggle for everyone, and no one meets all of life's challenges flawlessly.

At this time, please consider what you've read and learned, and journal your own personal response to this. This can be of great help in the future to see how you are progressing and changing.

2. Is GOD really in control of whatever happens?

There is some comfort in the realization that we are not alone in our suffering, but this is not enough to break the bands that bind us unless we also know that we are not subject to the power of impersonal fate or blind chance, no 'happenstance' or 'coincidence', we are in the hands of our Loving FATHER in Heaven.

1 Chronicles 29:11-12 ~ [11] Yours, O LORD, is the greatness and the power and the glory and the victory and the majesty, indeed everything that is in the heavens and the earth; Yours is the dominion, O LORD, and You exalt Yourself as head over all. [12] Both riches and honor *come* from You, and You rule over all, and in Your hand is power and might; and it lies in Your hand to make great and to strengthen everyone.

"The so-called great ones of this world, from Nebuchadnezzar to Mao Tse-tung--who lull themselves with the illusion that men create history cannot spoil God's plans, but instead they form an unwitting part of His plans and must serve His purposes even unconsciously and unwillingly. The tender mercy of God rings out like a bell over our dark world. And this theme sets itself against the riddles of our fate and against all human powers who rebel against it and pretend to be the lords of this world." ~ H. Thielicke

Matthew 10:29-30 ~ [29] Are not two sparrows sold for a cent? And *yet* not one of them will fall to the ground apart from your Father. [30] But the very hairs of your head are all numbered.

Isaiah 46:9-10 ~ [9] "Remember the former things long past, for I am God, and there is no other; *I am* God, and there is no one like Me, [10] Declaring the end from the beginning, and from ancient times things which have not been done, saying, 'My purpose will be established, and I will accomplish all My good pleasure'

Ephesians 1:11-12 ~ [11] also we have obtained an inheritance, having been predestined according to His purpose who works all things after the counsel of His will, [12] to the end that we who were the first to hope in Christ would be to the praise of His glory.

"God is never in a panic, nothing can be done that He is not absolute Master of, and no one in earth or heaven can shut a door He has opened, nor open a door He has shut. God alters the inevitable when we get in touch with Him." ~ O. Chambers

At this time, please consider what you've read and learned, and journal your own personal response to this. This can be of great help in the future to see how you are progressing and changing.

3. Where does sin come from?

Mark 7:21-23 ~ [21] For from within, out of the heart of men, proceed the evil thoughts, fornications, thefts, murders, adulteries, [22] deeds of coveting *and* wickedness, *as well as* deceit, sensuality, envy, slander, pride *and* foolishness. [23] All these evil things proceed from within and defile the man."

G. K. Chesterton, a philosopher, says that the great problem of philosophy is figuring out why little Tommy loves to torture the cat.

Thomas Malcolm Muggeridge, an English journalist and socialist, says that original sin, the most unpopular of all Christian dogmas, is the only one you can prove by the daily newspaper.

John 8:42-45 ~ [42] Jesus said to them, "If God were your Father, you would love Me, for I proceeded forth and have come from God, for I have not even come on My own initiative, but He sent Me. [43] Why do you not understand what I am saying? *It is* because you cannot hear My word. [44] You are of *your* father the devil, and you want to do the desires of your father. He was a murderer from the beginning and does not stand in the truth because there is no truth in him. Whenever he speaks a lie, he speaks from his own *nature*, for he is a liar and the father of lies. [45] But because I speak the truth, you do not believe Me.

"Sin has the devil for its father, shame for its companion, and death for its wages." ~ Thomas Watson

Romans 8:7-8 ~ [7] because the mind set on the flesh is hostile toward God; for it does not subject itself to the law of God, for it is not even able *to do so*, [8] and those who are in the flesh cannot please God.

Ephesians 2:1-3 ~ [1] And you were dead in your trespasses and sins, [2] in which you formerly walked according to the course of this world, according to the prince of the power of the air, of the spirit that is now working in the sons of disobedience. [3] Among them we too all formerly lived in the lusts of our flesh, indulging the desires of the flesh and of the mind, and were by nature children of wrath, even as the rest.

"All three evils, sin and death and suffering, are from us, not from God; from our misuse of our free will, from our disobedience. We started it!" ~ P. Kreeft

"We are sinners. Our world is a battlefield strewn with broken treaties, broken families, broken promises, broken lives, and broken hearts. We are good stuff gone bad, a defaced masterpiece, a rebellious child." ~ P. Kreeft

At this time, please consider what you've read and learned, and journal your own personal response to this. This can be of great help in the future to see how you are progressing and changing.

4. Can GOD overrule sin?

Romans 8:28 ~ [28] And we know that God causes all things to work together for good to those who love God, to those who are called according to *His* purpose.

Joseph's brothers were jealous of him, hated him, plotted to murder him, sold him into slavery, told his father he was dead, and abandoned him to his fate. But GOD made him second to Pharaoh over Egypt and used him to save his family from starvation. His brothers feared that he would take vengeance on them. He gave one reason why he would not do so in these words...

Genesis 50:20 ~ As for you, you meant evil against me, *but* God meant it for good in order to bring about this present result, to preserve many people alive.

"What his brothers did was genuinely significant--and hurt Joseph deeply. But Joseph had eyes to see that God was also at work, and that His purposes had been fulfilled not just in spite of his brothers, but even through their actions!" ~ S. B. Ferguson

Acts 2:22-24 ~ [22] "Men of Israel, listen to these words: Jesus the Nazarene, a man attested to you by God with miracles and wonders and signs which God performed through Him in your midst, just as you yourselves know [23] this *Man*, delivered over by the predetermined plan and foreknowledge of God, you nailed to a cross by the hands of godless men and put *Him* to death. [24] But God raised Him up again, putting an end to the agony of death, since it was impossible for Him to be held in its power.

Acts 3:13-15 ~ [13] The God of Abraham, Isaac and Jacob, the God of our fathers, has glorified His servant Jesus, *the one* whom you delivered and disowned in the presence of Pilate, when he had decided to release Him. [14] But you disowned the Holy and Righteous One and asked for a murderer to be granted to you, [15] but put to death the Prince of life, *the one* whom God raised from the dead, *a fact* to which we are witnesses.

"The sentence which Jesus' human judges passed upon Him and His human executioners carried out has been reversed, Peter asserts, by a higher court. They put Him to death, but God raised Him up." ~ F. F. Bruce

Acts 3:26 ~ For you first, God raised up His Servant and sent Him to bless you by turning every one *of you* from your wicked ways.

The greatest tragedy in the world, the death of JESUS The CHRIST, is also the greatest Blessing in the world! It can be the way sinners are Saved! YAHWEH, GOD Almighty, can turn the worst into the best!

At this time, please consider what you've read and learned, and journal your own personal response to this. This can be of great help in the future to see how you are progressing and changing.

5. Does GOD really Love me?

Psalm 86:15 ~ But You, O Lord, are a God merciful and gracious, slow to anger and abundant in lovingkindness and truth.

A woman who had lived her life totally without reference to God was told by a doctor that her daughter, who had been injured in an automobile accident, would probably never come out of the coma and could quite possibly remain in the coma the rest of her life.

The woman said, "I walked out of the hospital and across the street to a bar and got totally zonkered. Then I got into my car and drove home, weeping the whole way. When I got in my driveway, I turned off the engine and began to curse God. I used every bit of vile language I knew, and I knew a lot. After about a half hour I was totally drained. And in the silence, I heard a voice and the voice said, 'That is the first time you have ever spoken to Me, and I love you.'"

Psalm 145:8-9 ~ [8] The LORD is gracious and merciful; Slow to anger and great in lovingkindness. [9] The LORD is good to all, and His mercies are over all His works.

"Jesus Christ reveals, not an embarrassed God, not a confused God, not a God who stands apart from the problems, but One who stands in the thick of the whole thing with man." ~ O. Chambers

1 John 3:16 ~ We know love by this, that He laid down His life for us; and we ought to lay down our lives for the brethren.

"It is quite natural (but wrong) to think that we have to become worthy in order for God to accept us. This harmful perception keeps people from coming to Christ, for it leads them to believe that He died for some sinners but not others. Homosexuals and adulterers, along with all of us, must bask in the love of God; we all must be willing to open our lives to His grace. God does not turn His back on those who believe in His Son." ~ E. W. Lutzer

1 John 4:16 ~ We have come to know and have believed the love which God has for us. God is love, and the one who abides in love abides in God, and God abides in him.

"How you view God determines the quality and style of your Christian experience. Many Christians spend much of their lives paralyzed because, although they have trusted Christ as Savior, they have never really seen what His sacrifice teaches us about the character of God. He gave His Son because He loves us. He thereby proves His grace. Do you know God, in this way?" ~ S. Ferguson

1 John 4:19 ~ We love, because He first loved us.

"The people of God have ground for cheerfulness. They are justified and adopted, and this creates music within whatever storms are without." ~ Thomas Watson

At this time, please consider what you've read and learned, and journal your own personal response to this. This can be of great help in the future to see how you are progressing and changing.

6. Does suffering have a purpose?

Romans 5:3-4 ~ [3] And not only this, but we also exult in our tribulations, knowing that tribulation brings about perseverance; [4] and perseverance, proven character; and proven character, hope

"Blessed is that hour of holy desperation when a man moves out of the wreck of himself and into Christ." ~ V. Havner

2Corinthians 1:3-4 ~ [3] Blessed *be* the God and Father of our Lord Jesus Christ, the Father of mercies and God of all comfort, [4] who comforts us in all our affliction so that we will be able to comfort those who are in any affliction with the comfort with which we ourselves are comforted by God.

"I often feel very grateful to God that I have undergone fearful depression. I know the borders of despair and the horrible brink of that gulf of darkness into which my feet have almost gone. But hundreds of times I have been able to give a helpful grip to brethren who have come into that same condition, which grip I could never have given if I had not known their deep despondency. So I believe that the darkest and most dreadful experience of a child of God will help him if he will but follow Christ." ~ C. H. Spurgeon

James 1:2-4 ~ [2] Consider it all joy, my brethren, when you encounter various trials, [3] knowing that the testing of your faith produces endurance. [4] And let endurance have *its* perfect result, so that you may be perfect and complete, lacking in nothing.

I read of a young man, that was a Christian, who struggled a lot with his homosexual nature. He could never remember a time when he had been attracted to girls. He'd found himself falling in love with males since childhood. He had never engaged in homosexual sex. He did not want to be homosexual.

He'd have given anything to change his sexual desires, and he knew little of the Holy Spirit's power to do this. He made all of his agony into material to be a better Christian witness, telling us why he could not deny his Savior by following his desires.

Whenever I grow discouraged, that discouragement is my evidence that I am doubting that YAHWEH, GOD Almighty, is in charge of my life, that HE Loves me, that HE intends to use me to further HIS Kingdom, and that HE intends to Bless others through me.

At this time, please consider what you've read and learned, and journal your own personal response to this. This can be of great help in the future to see how you are progressing and changing.

7. Can GOD really bring good out of trouble?

Psalm 119:71 ~ It is good for me that I was afflicted, that I may learn Your statutes.

Many times we do not understand that the hurt is allowed to come so that we can appreciate the healing, as well as The Healer! AMen!!

"Trial is not only to approve, but to improve." ~ Thomas Manton IV

"The tears of the godly are sweeter than the triumph of the wicked." ~ Thomas Watson

Romans 8:28 ~ And we know that God causes all things to work together for good to those who love God, to those who are called according to *His* purpose.

A devout Christian young man lamented that he just couldn't let go of bitterness he felt about certain mental wounds he had suffered years earlier. He could quote Scriptures about how he should forgive, but he still didn't feel forgiving. He had prayed repeatedly, 'Thank you God, for letting such-and-such happen in my life.' Still, he didn't feel thankful.

Then he used the idea that one picture is worth a thousand words. He pictured the wrongs done to him as gashes cutting deeply into his body. Then he imagined himself to be a giant key, and those gashes took on new meaning. They became notches precisely machined along the edge of the key to make it uniquely useful.

God could use him as a tool to fit locks that no other key could budge. The locks represented bitterness, discouragement, fear, and much more deep within the minds of others.

Now he, the notched key, could understand them. The hurts in his life had made him useful to other people's lives. He wept and laughed as he visualized God's huge hands turning him, the key, in those locks and freeing others from their emotional prisons.

I can identify with this greatly! My Hope, and Prayer, is for you to also one day be "a key" that helps unlock someone else's deepest and darkest misery! That helps to set them Free. AMen

2Corinthians 4:17 ~ For momentary, light affliction is producing for us an eternal weight of glory far beyond all comparison

Hebrews 12:11 ~ All discipline for the moment seems not to be joyful, but sorrowful; yet to those who have been trained by it, afterwards it yields the peaceful fruit of righteousness

At this time, please consider what you've read and learned, and journal your own personal response to this. This can be of great help in the future to see how you are progressing and changing.

8. Should GOD'S children ignore, or refuse, self-pity?

Self-pity is a fertile seed-bed, where all types of temptation blossom with deep roots which are very difficult to pull up.

Philippians 2:14 ~ Do all things without grumbling or disputing

"If we can recognize the pain that we must endure as wind in our sails, we will use the agony rather than curse it." ~ R. A. Williams

Philippians 4:11-13 ~ [11] Not that I speak from want, for I have learned to be content in whatever circumstances I am. [12] I know how to get along with humble means, and I also know how to live in prosperity; in any and every circumstance I have learned the secret of being filled and going hungry, both of having abundance and suffering need. [13] I can do all things through Him who strengthens me.

"The game of life is not so much in holding a good hand as playing a poor hand well." ~ H. T. Leslie

Jude 1:14-16 ~ [14] *It was* also about these men *that* Enoch, *in* the seventh *generation* from Adam, prophesied, saying, "Behold, the Lord came with many thousands of His holy ones, [15] to execute judgment upon all, and to convict all the ungodly of all their ungodly deeds which they have done in an ungodly way, and of all the harsh things which ungodly sinners have spoken against Him." [16] These are grumblers, finding fault, following after their *own* lusts; they speak arrogantly, flattering people for the sake of *gaining an* advantage.

"Because sin deserves death and we are all sinners, all our mercies are undeserved mercies. Any apparent unfairness in God's treatment of us arises not because some have too much punishment, but because some of us appear to have too little. None of us will ever receive harsher judgment than we deserve. The marvel is, in the biblical view, not that men die for their sins, but that we remain alive in spite of them." ~ J. W. Wenham

At this time, please consider what you've read and learned, and journal your own personal response to this. This can be of great help in the future to see how you are progressing and changing.

9. How can I live this life of Praise?

Psalm 9:9-10 ~ [9] The LORD also will be a stronghold for the oppressed, A stronghold in times of trouble; [10] And those who know Your name will put their trust in You, for You, O LORD, have not forsaken those who seek You.

Dr. John Claypool lost his young daughter to leukemia. As he watched his little girl suffer, he could see no reason for what was happening to her. He understood how a man could turn against God and at times was not far from doing so himself. But he did not succumb.

Instead, he responds, "If we are willing, the experience of grief can deepen and widen our ability to participate in life. We can become more grateful for the gifts we have been given, more open-handed in our handling of the events of life, more sensitive to the whole mysterious process of life, and more trusting in our adventure with God."

Psalm 30:4-5 ~ [4] Sing praise to the LORD, you His godly ones, And give thanks to His holy name. [5] For His anger is but for a moment, His favor is for a lifetime; Weeping may last for the night, but a shout of joy *comes* in the morning.

"In hours of pain and grief we learn in Him unfaltering faith and trust, only because we will and not because we must." ~ W. O. Carver

Psalm 34:22 ~ The LORD redeems the soul of His servants, and none of those who take refuge in Him will be condemned.

"Grace's worst is better than the world's best." ~ Thomas Manton IV

Proverbs 30:5 ~ Every word of God is tested; He is a shield to those who take refuge in Him.

"Two children were playing on a hillside, when they noticed the hour was nearing sunset, and one said wonderingly: 'See how far the sun has gone! A little while ago it was right over that tree, and now it is low down in the sky.' 'Only it isn't the sun that moves; it's the earth. Father told us,' said the other. The first one shook his head. The sun did move, for he had seen it, and the earth did not move for he had been standing on it all the time. 'I know what I see,' he said triumphantly. 'And I believe Father,' said his brother. So, mankind divides today-- some accepting only what their senses reveal to them, the others believing the Word of God." ~ W. B. Knight

Isaiah 26:3-4 ~ 3 "The steadfast of mind You will keep in perfect peace, because he trusts in You. 4 "Trust in the LORD forever, for in GOD the LORD, *we have* an everlasting Rock.

"It is not miserable to be blind; it is miserable to be incapable of enduring blindness." ~ J. Milton

Romans 8:35-37 ~ 35 Who shall separate us from the love of CHRIST? shall tribulation, or distress, or persecution, or famine, or nakedness, or peril, or sword? 36 As it is written, for thy sake we are killed all the day long; we are accounted as sheep for the slaughter. 37 Nay, in all these things we are more than conquerors through him that loved us.

W. R. Maltby wrote, "In the sermon on the mount, Jesus promised His disciples three things --that they would be entirely fearless, absurdly happy, and that they would get into trouble. They did get into trouble, and found, to their surprise, that they were not afraid. They were absurdly happy, for they laughed over their own troubles, and only cried over other peoples'."

"Was His head crowned with thorns, and do we think to be crowned with roses?" ~ Thomas Watson

Romans 15:13 ~ Now may the God of hope fill you with all joy and peace in believing, so that you will abound in hope by the power of the Holy Spirit.

"God is the Creator of the universe, the Comforter of the sorrowing." ~ Thomas Watson

At this time, please consider what you've read and learned, and journal your own personal response to this. This can be of great help in the future to see how you are progressing and changing.

10. Who brought all sin and misery into the world?

2Corinthians 11:3 ~ But I am afraid that, as the serpent deceived Eve by his craftiness, your minds will be led astray from the simplicity and purity *of devotion* to Christ.

"You all know the father of sin, that is, the devil. The devil is the father, lust the mother, consent the midwife, and custom the nurse; if consent bring it forth, custom will bring it up." ~ T. Adams

Ephesians 6:12 ~ For our struggle is not against flesh and blood, but against the rulers, against the powers, against the world forces of this darkness, against the spiritual *forces* of wickedness in the heavenly *places*.

Always remember that Satan and his minions are out to disable the body, deceive the mind, and discourage the spirit. He attacks through morals, through the mind, through moods. Thoughts and feelings!

There is no war going on between GOD Almighty and the devil! That war has been won at The Cross! The battle is the enemy trying to win each of us over to his rebellion.

1John 3:8 ~ the one who practices sin is of the devil; for the devil has sinned from the beginning. The Son of God appeared for this purpose, to destroy the works of the devil.

1Peter 5:8 ~ Be of sober *spirit*, be on the alert. Your adversary, the devil, prowls around like a roaring lion, seeking someone to devour.

Do not let the evil one persuade you that you can have any secrets. Transparency is key. Speak it, confess it, and it holds no more power over you!

Revelation 12:9 ~ And the great dragon was thrown down, the serpent of old who is called the devil and Satan, who deceives the whole world; he was thrown down to the earth, and his angels were thrown down with him.

While the devil is popularly depicted as some man with horns, tail, and pitchfork, masking the dreadful reality of evil, the Bible plainly exposes him. It uses many names to describe Satan because he is terribly complex and appears in many forms in real life.

He will appear as everything you've ever desired, but do not need.

devil = the accuser or slanderer (Job 1:6-11, 2:1-7; Revelation 12:10). In Hebrew Satan means adversary.

At this time, please consider what you've read and learned, and journal your own personal response to this. This can be of great help in the future to see how you are progressing and changing.

11. Has the devil's power and that of all his hosts been broken at the Cross?

Genesis 3:14-15 ~ [14] The LORD God said to the serpent, "Because you have done this, cursed are you more than all cattle, And more than every beast of the field; On your belly you will go, and dust you will eat all the days of your life; [15] And I will put enmity between you and the woman, and between your seed and her seed; He shall bruise you on the head, and you shall bruise him on the heel."

"The monumental importance of this verse has been recognized by commentators from ancient times. Its gospel character is so marked that for centuries it has been known as the 'protoevangel," i.e., 'first gospel,' for it is the first hint of the good news." ~ F. Gaebelein

Here, at the very beginning of Scripture is the central teaching of God's Word. Here we have "the one great central Truth of all prophecy--the coming of One, Who, though HE should suffer, would in the end crush the head of the old serpent (the devil).

Matthew 12:28-29 ~ [28] But if I cast out demons by the Spirit of God, then the kingdom of God has come upon you. [29] Or how can anyone enter the strong man's house and carry off his property, unless he first binds the strong *man*? And then he will plunder his house.

YESHUA, JESUS The CHRIST, right here, answers the slander of the Pharisees who had said that HE cast out devils by Beelzebub, the prince of the devils.

HE shows the absurdity of the accusation by comparing the power of the devil with that of a kingdom or a town or a house. If one devil should cast out another, the kingdom of the devils would not stand but would fall asunder. But this does not happen. That is why there is only one explanation for JESUS' Power over the demons, JESUS was fully Man and fully GOD.

JESUS' superior power over satan is already proven at the start by the temptation in the wilderness. JESUS' rejection of the temptation is already the beginning of HIS Victory and of the coming of the kingdom, although this victory will have to be renewed again and again during HIS life on earth.

The powers of hell were finally smashed at the Cross and this Victory will be fully consummated when JESUS returns.

John 12:31-33 ~ [31] Now judgment is upon this world; now the ruler of this world will be cast out. [32] And I, if I am lifted up from the earth, will draw all men to Myself." [33] But He was saying this to indicate the kind of death by which He was to die.

Superficial views of The Gospel produce superficial Christians!

Colossians 2:13-15 ~ [13] When you were dead in your transgressions and the uncircumcision of your flesh, He made you alive together with Him, having forgiven us all our transgressions, [14] having canceled out the certificate of debt consisting of decrees against us, which was hostile to us; and He has taken it out of the way, having nailed it to the cross. [15] When He had disarmed the rulers and authorities, He made a public display of them, having triumphed over them through

Him.

Some may ask, "If the power of satan and his hosts was broken at the Cross, then why do I have such difficulty finding Freedom from my strongholds and addictions? Why are my struggles so painful? Why do I sometimes fail?"

Satan's plans were demolished at Calvary and his doom is certain. We have the Hope of eternal salvation. There are still battles to be fought, but Freedom is ours in JESUS The CHRIST as we endure til the end! The power of those strongholds has already been broken at the Cross!

JESUS was crucified on The Cross, this ole flesh was not!

At this time, please consider what you've read and learned, and journal your own personal response to this. This can be of great help in the future to see how you are progressing and changing.

12. What kind of battle am I fighting?

2 Corinthians 10:3-5 ~ [3] For though we walk in the flesh, we do not war according to the flesh, [4] for the weapons of our warfare are not of the flesh, but divinely powerful for the destruction of fortresses. [5] *We are* destroying speculations and every lofty thing raised up against the knowledge of God, and *we are* taking every thought captive to the obedience of Christ

Never ever try to deal with temptation by yourself, bring GOD into the battle. This is done by also recognizing that HIS Spirit dwells within HIS People... utilize them.

The weapons of our warfare are spiritual, not carnal. They have been supplied by the life, death, and resurrection of our LORD & SAVIOR. As we learn to use the weapons HE has provided, we overcome the evil one. For us, the issue is no longer sin, but Faith! We must ask ourselves, "Will I continue to pray without ceasing, 'Please help me overcome my addiction, my stronghold, my vice, my lust and desire,' or will I say boldly by Faith, 'Thank YOU, LORD, that you have already smashed the power of that stronghold at the cross'?"

We know that satan is the master of illusion. When we stumble, it is because we believe his lies instead of believing GOD'S Truth. In this warfare he uses four big guns: condemnation, sin, law, and death. These can only be spiked by Faith--Fighting Faith!

1Timothy 6:12 ~ Fight the good fight of faith, lay hold on eternal life, whereunto thou are also called, and have professed a good profession before many witnesses.

The individual who is not anchored in JESUS can offer no resistance on his own resources to the physical and moral flattery and lust of the world.

Revelation 12:11 ~ And they overcame him by the blood of the Lamb and by the word of their testimony, and they loved not their lives unto the death.

At this time, please consider what you've read and learned, and journal your own personal response to this. This can be of great help in the future to see how you are progressing and changing.

13. Was the power of addiction, strongholds and sin to shame us broken at the Cross?

Some might say, "I can see how the devil could use the guns of condemnation and sin to trouble GOD'S Children, but how can he use GOD'S Law as a weapon? Isn't the law 'Holy, and Just, and Good' (Romans 7:12)?" It is, but the law must be used lawfully (1Timothy 1:8)!

The law can tell us what is right or wrong, but Scripture tells us that it is "weak through the flesh" (Romans 8:3). It cannot forgive the offender or empower the helpless.

The law was not given as the way of deliverance, but in order "that every mouth may be stopped, and all the world may become guilty before GOD. By the law is the knowledge of sin" (Romans 3:19-20). The law never justifies people (Galatians 2:16; 3:11); it was given to lead people to CHRIST (Galatians 3:24). Those who are under the law need redemption, and JESUS came to be under the law to redeem those who were under the law (Galatians 4:4-5).

Therefore, while we should look to the law to teach us right from wrong, we must not look to the law for righteousness or strength. The law is not our LORD. The law is not our SAVIOR! We must look only to YESHUA, JESUS The CHRIST, for the removal of our guilt and for all our righteousness (John 1:29 and Philippians 3:8-9). We must look only to the HOLY SPIRIT for power and guidance (Acts 1:8).

Condemnation brings the sinners heart to repentance, but it does not save!

Acts 13:38-39 ~ [38] Therefore let it be known to you, brethren, that through Him forgiveness of sins is proclaimed to you, [39] and through Him everyone who believes is freed from all things, from which you could not be freed through the Law of Moses.

"This does not mean that the Law of Moses justified from some things, but Jesus from more. Rather, the meaning is 'forgiveness for everything--which the law never offered'" ~ L. Morris

Justification is basically a legal term and it means more than pardon. It indicates that the person concerned is treated as innocent, as having been acquitted at the bar of GOD'S Justice. The death of JESUS is the means of conferring on us the status of being righteous in GOD'S sight.

Romans 7:4 ~ [4] Therefore, my brethren, you also were made to die to the Law through the body of Christ, so that you might be joined to another, to Him who was raised from the dead, in order that we might bear fruit for God.

Romans 10:4 ~ For Christ is the end of the law for righteousness to everyone who believes.

Galatians 2:16 ~ [16] nevertheless knowing that a man is not justified by the works of the Law but through faith in Christ Jesus, even we have believed in Christ Jesus, so that we may be justified by faith in Christ and not by the works of the Law; since by the works of the Law no flesh will be justified.

"The law commands and makes us know what duties to our God we owe; but 'tis the gospel must reveal where lies our strength to do His will. The law discovers guilt and sin, and shows how vile our hearts have been; only the gospel can express forgiving love and cleansing grace. What curses does the law denounce against the man that fails but once! But in the gospel Christ appears, pardoning the guilt of numerous years. My soul, no more attempt to draw Thy life and comfort from the law: fly to the hope the gospel gives: the man that trusts the promise, lives." ~ I. Watts

Galatians 3:10-13 ~ [10] For as many as are of the works of the Law are under a curse; for it is written, "CURSED IS EVERYONE WHO DOES NOT ABIDE BY ALL THINGS WRITTEN IN THE BOOK OF THE LAW, TO PERFORM THEM."

[11] Now that no one is justified by the Law before God is evident; for, "THE RIGHTEOUS MAN SHALL LIVE BY FAITH." [12] However, the Law is not of faith; on the contrary, "HE WHO PRACTICES THEM SHALL LIVE BY THEM."

[13] Christ redeemed us from the curse of the Law, having become a curse for us—for it is written, "CURSED IS EVERYONE WHO HANGS ON A TREE"

When strong temptations come over us, we experience anxiety, confusion, and depression. We wonder what we really want. We feel guilty and worthless and fear that we will never be what we ought to be.

If we surrender to all this, we will inevitably begin to say, "It's no use! I'll never make it. I'm a failure. Why fight any longer?" Faith, however, fights back, using the Word of GOD.

At this time, please consider what you've read and learned, and journal your own personal response to this. This can be of great help in the future to see how you are progressing and changing.

14. Can GOD restore what sin has marred?

2Corinthians 5:17 ~ [17] Therefore if anyone is in Christ, *he is* a new creature; the old things passed away; behold, new things have come.

Galatians 6:9 ~ [9] Let us not lose heart in doing good, for in due time we will reap if we do not grow weary.

Teach us, GoOD LORD, to serve THEE!

Teach us, GOoD LORD, to give and not to count the cost!

Teach us, GoOD LORD, to fight and not to heed the wounds!

Teach us, Oh LORD, to toil and not to ask for rest!

Teach us, my LORD, my SAVIOR, to labor and not to ask for any reward save knowing that we do YOUR Will!

At this time, please consider what you've read and learned, and journal your own personal response to this. This can be of great help in the future to see how you are progressing and changing.

Becoming a Christian does not mean that our Faith is perfect or always strong. All too often we fail to take advantage of the treasures of Grace that are available to us through the finished work of YESHUA, JESUS The CHRIST, on The Cross.

This is especially true in times of strong temptation when our habitual emotional responses come into play and the devil uses the old feelings of guilt, shame and fear to stampede us away from the path of GOD.

It is important to remember in times of temptation that these strongholds, addictions, habits, do bring suffering. I am still not fully immune to the hardships of temptation.

There are times of intense loneliness when the enemy whispers, "I am your only chance for love. Yield or you will be forever alone." And I say aloud, Amen! Thank YOU, JESUS, that YOU truly are my only chance for Love! For Truth! For Freedom! It is then that I hear the promise, "I can ease your pain and banish the hurt."

It is vital to remember the pain that our strongholds, our addictions, our sin, has caused each of us in the past so that we can discern the lie it tries to tell us now.

Me personally, I need to remember how homosexuality and transgenderism took my self-respect and gave me guilt, took my honor and gave me shame, took my honesty and made me a lie, took my gentleness and made me an angry man that set out to intentionally and purposely infect as many as possible with HIV.

I need to remember that it led me to betray my GOD, my friends, all those who trusted me. I need to remember how it promised relief but gave only pain; promised love but gave only lust and loneliness. I need to remember how it robbed me and almost destroyed my sanity and my life, both physically and spiritually.

But it is also important to remember that GOD does bring good out of trouble. Otherwise sorrow will swallow me up and give fresh power to temptation.

I need to remember that, just as physical pain warns the body to get out of harm's way, so emotional pain is GOD'S "early warning system" crying, "This is not the way. Walk ye not in it." By it HE positions me for Grace.

Only those who labor and are heavy laden will come to HIM for rest (Matthew 11:28-30). HE does not delight in the pain or the sin which is its source. HE does overrule to bring good out of all our troubles as we, and only if we, walk with HIM in HIS Way. The Way.

Helpful Hints

1) Write out all the ways you know unwanted sexual desires and lusts caused you pain in your journal. Then write all the ways GOD has or can bring good out of these troubles. Share what you have written and begin, by Faith, to Praise GOD for the Blessings which are or will be yours.

2) Read aloud Psalm 103 every morning when you awake and every evening before you go to sleep, and Praise GOD for HIS loving, gracious sovereignty over all that comes to you.

3) Memorize one of the verses you found helpful in this chapter.

4) Write an account of your most recent, serious struggle in your journal. Which 'guns' did the devil use against you-- condemnation, sin, law, and/or death? How did he use them? How did you respond? How do you plan to respond when he strikes next (because he will strike again)?

Method 3. Accept the fact that our intended identity is found only, in YESHUA, JESUS The CHRIST.

Purpose 3. To be able to Trust our FATHER in Heaven, confident that it will bring us into a familiar and familial bond with HIM, and our brethren (brothers & sisters). Intimacy!

Who is the real me? That question has haunted many of us for years. Strongholds, addictions, habits and misidentified desires have all led each one of us into a severe identity crisis.

Where do we learn our true identity? We cannot expect our thoughts and feelings to provide the answer to that question because our past experiences have distorted them. Nor can we trust friends or family who share those same thoughts and feelings, those same falsehoods.

It is okay to be afraid of the fact that others who have not experienced our struggle cannot understand. So, who can we wisely and safely trust to show us who we are?

John Calvin said, "It is certain that man never achieves a clear knowledge of himself unless he has first looked upon GOD'S Face, and then descends from contemplating HIM to scrutinize himself."

GOD made our first parents in HIS Image (Genesis 1:26-27). They knew HIM, understood themselves and were comfortable with each other. However, sin changed all that.

In place of the beauty which GOD intended came all the horrors humanity now knows. When we look at people in general, and at ourselves in particular, we no longer see the pure likeness of GOD.

We behold a mass of problems like cruelty, apathy, hatred, resentment, indifference, bitterness, rage, lust, rebellion, greed, immorality, envy, pride, deception, perversion, lasciviousness and a thousand other tragic deformities and misidentifications.

Created in the image of YAHWEH, GOD Almighty. Born in the image of Adam. Born into sin, shaped in iniquity. The word iniquity is rooted from "perversion". We are born into sin and shaped in perversion.

The Bible tells us that homosexuality, sodomy, bestiality, necrophilia and the list goes on, are all distortions of HIS very intention of Creation. Scripture teaches that GOD'S Plan was for the sexual union of male and female (Genesis 2:24), not for the union of two males or two females (Leviticus 18:22-23 & Romans 1:26-27).

The Bible also teaches us that such acts are "not natural" and can only lead to death (Romans 1:26-31). And being unnatural, goes against GOD'S Created and intended purpose for mankind. Homosexuality is a direct and deliberate attack against GOD'S very thought, or intention, of Creating one man and one woman.

Something has happened to us that led us to diverge from our original purpose. Where did we go wrong? How can we get back there? These are the questions which we need to answer. These are the questions that can reveal our intended identity in YESHUA, JESUS The CHRIST.

We must first understand that distorted ideas about GOD lead to a twisted concept of self. We begin by seeking HIS Face; how do we do that?

Through The Scriptures that introduce us to HIM. We find, as we seek, that GOD is not a distant ogre or a harsh tyrant; but a Loving FATHER Who forgives and accepts each one of us in spite of all that we have done or have/had become! We also discover that HE is our Sovereign LORD Who is working all things for HIS GoOD! HE is also our Mighty SAVIOR Who has delivered us from sin and from the enemy's clutches at a great cost!

As we begin to better understand our FATHER through HIS Word, we must begin to better understand ourselves. First, we must understand and then face the lies that we have accepted. Then we embrace the Truth.

1. What is one source of the longings we sometimes feel?

Psalm 42:1-2 ~ [1] As the deer pants for the water brooks, so my soul pants for You, O God. [2] My soul thirsts for God, for the living God; When shall I come and appear before God?

HE has formed us for HIMSELF, and our hearts are restless till they find rest in HIM.

Though we may have trusted in YESHUA, JESUS The CHRIST, and though we understand that we are completely Loved, Forgiven and Accepted; we may still keep HIM at a distance and look for fulfillment elsewhere because of our own fears and distortions that we have accepted as reality. And so, we risk missing true satisfaction.

Psalm 63:1-3 ~ [1] O God, Thou art my God; early will I seek Thee; my soul thirsteth for Thee; my flesh longeth for Thee in a dry and thirsty land, where no water is. [2] To see Thy power and Thy glory, so as I have seen Thee in the sanctuary. [3] Because Thy lovingkindness is better than life, my lips shall praise Thee.

"In comparison with this big world, the human heart is only a small thing. Though the world is so large, it is utterly unable to satisfy this tiny heart. Man's ever-growing soul and its capacities can be satisfied only in the infinite God." ~ S. Singh

Psalm 84:2 ~ My soul longeth, yea, even fainteth for the courts of the LORD: my heart and my flesh crieth out for the living God.

"The blank space in the modern heart", said Julian Huxley, "is a 'God-shaped blank.'"

"We may go with the bee from flower to flower, but we shall never have full satisfaction till we come to the infinite God." ~ Thomas Watson

At this time, please consider what you've read and learned, and journal your own personal response to this. This can be of great help in the future to see how you are progressing and changing.

2. What is GOD'S attitude toward man now?

John 3:16 ~ For God so loved the world, that He gave His only begotten Son, that whoever believes in Him shall not perish, but have eternal life.

We have an Almighty Loving GOD that Loved the world so much that HE robed HIMSELF in flesh, came to this world as the Man YESHUA, JESUS The CHRIST to be the ransom for our sin; for our wrong doings!!! Let that sink in.

Romans 1:18 ~ For the wrath of God is revealed from heaven against all ungodliness and unrighteousness of men who suppress the truth in unrighteousness

The Bible speaks of GOD'S Wrath but assures us that GOD is Love, always and unchangeably (1John 4:8; Malachi 3:6; Hebrews 13:8). How can both be true? Since GOD Loves us, HE must react against the sin that is destructive to us and others.

Scripture teaches that GOD'S Wrath is revealed in handing men and women over to the full force of sin (Romans 1).

At this time, please consider what you've read and learned, and journal your own personal response to this. This can be of great help in the future to see how you are progressing and changing.

3. Has GOD revealed HIMSELF to humankind?

Psalm 19:1-3 ~ The heavens are telling of the glory of God; And their expanse is declaring the work of His hands. [2] Day to day pours forth speech, and night to night reveals knowledge. [3] There is no speech, nor are there words; Their voice is not heard.

"An atheist is a man who believes himself an accident." ~ F. Thompson

Romans 1:19-20 ~ [19] Because that which may be known of God is manifest in them; for God hath shewed it unto them. [20] For the invisible things of him from the creation of the world are clearly seen, being understood by the things that are made, even his eternal power and Godhead; so that they are without excuse

A young soldier, by the name of Larry Maggard, sent this poem to his mother in a letter that arrived the same day as the telegram notifying his parents of his death:

**'Lord God, I have never spoken to you,
But now I want to say: How do you do?
You see, God, they told me you didn't exist,
And like a fool, I believed all this.**

'Last night from a shell hole I saw your sky;
I figured right then they had told me a lie,
Had I taken time to see things you made
I'd have known they weren't calling a spade a spade.

'I wonder, God, if you'll take my hand,
Somehow I feel that you'll understand.
Funny I had to come to this hellish place
Before I had time to see your face.

'Well, I guess there isn't much more to say,
But I'm sure glad, God, I met you today.
I guess zero hour will soon be here,
But I'm not afraid since I know you're near.

'The signal! Well God, I'll have to go.
I like you lots, I want you to know.
Look, now, this will be a horrible fight,
Who knows, I may come to your house tonight.

'Tho' I wasn't friendly to you before,
I wonder, God, if you'd wait at Your door.
Look, I'm crying! Me shedding tears!
I wish I'd known you these many years.

Well, I'll have to go now, God. Goodbye.
Strange how, since I met you, I'm not afraid to die!'"

There are beautiful, majestic mountains, blue-gray in the distance, massive and enduring. Amazingly colorful and bright skylines that are never the same, but yet so overwhelmingly creative. Plants, trees, and flowers all around us that scream for attention in their gorgeous, delicate and intricate design.

Once in a while someone who claims they do not believe in GOD Almighty will admit that if you look at these things all around us long enough, you start to suspect there's something out there greater than you!

"When Helen Keller (who had been rendered permanently blind and deaf by illness at the age of nineteen months) was 10 years of age, her father asked Phillips Brooks to tell her about God. Gladly he did so, and the two corresponded as long as he lived. Brooks was profoundly impressed with the remark she made after the first conversation, that she had always known there was a God, but had not before known His name." ~ A. W. Blackwood

Romans 2:14-15 ~ [14] For when the Gentiles, which have not the law, do by nature the things contained in the law, these, having not the law, are a law unto themselves: [15] Which shew the work of the law written in their hearts, their conscience also bearing witness, and their thoughts the mean while accusing or else excusing one another

"Two things fill the mind with ever-increasing wonder and awe, the more often and the more intensely the mind of thought is drawn to them: the starry heavens above me and the moral law within me." ~ I. Kant

2 Peter 1:19-21 ~ [19] We have also a more sure word of prophecy; whereunto ye do well that ye take heed, as unto a light that shineth in a dark place, until the day dawn, and the day star arise in your hearts: [20] Knowing this first, that no prophecy of the scripture is of any private interpretation. [21] For the prophecy came not in old time by the will of man: but holy men of God spoke as they were moved by the Holy Ghost.

"I want to know one thing, the way to heaven: how to land safe on that happy shore. God Himself has condescended to teach The Way; for this very end He came from heaven. He hath written it down in a book! I have it; here is knowledge enough for me. Let me be a man of one book. Here then I am, far from the busy ways of men. I sit down alone; only God is here. In His presence I open, I read this book. Is there a doubt concerning the meaning of what I read? Does anything appear dark or intricate? I lift up my heart to the Father of Lights. Lord, is it not Thy word, 'If any man lack wisdom, let him ask of God'? Thou has said, 'If any be willing to do Thy will, he shall know.' I am willing to do Thy will; let me know Thy will." ~ John Wesley

At this time, please consider what you've read and learned, and journal your own personal response to this. This can be of great help in the future to see how you are progressing and changing.

4. How has humanity responded to GOD?

Jeremiah 2:13 ~ "For My people have committed two evils: They have forsaken Me, the fountain of living waters, to hew for themselves cisterns, broken cisterns that can hold no water.

"It is natural for the mind to believe, and for the will to love; so that, for want of true objects, they must attach themselves to false." ~ B. Pascal

"You can hear it over and over again--all kinds of secondary solutions to secondary problems. Of course, these are problems, but they are not the central problem. The real reason we are in such a mess is that we have turned away from the God who is there and the Truth which He has revealed. The problem is that the house is so rotten that even smaller earthquakes shake it to the core." ~ F. Schaeffer

Romans 1:21-23 ~ [21] Because that, when they knew God, they glorified him not as God, neither were thankful; but became vain in their imaginations, and their foolish heart was darkened. [22] Professing themselves to be wise, they became fools, [23] And changed the glory of the uncorruptible God into an image made like to corruptible man, and to birds, and four-footed beasts, and creeping things.

"The fallen self cannot know itself. We do not know who we are and will search for an identity in someone or something other than God until we find ourselves in Him." ~ L. Payne

Romans 1:25 ~ Who changed the truth of God into a lie, and worshipped and served the creature more than the Creator, who is blessed forever. Amen.

"Our world lies on the brink of disaster because we as people have turned our backs on the God who made us. Our only hope is to turn back to Him--one life at a time." ~ R. S. Richards

At this time, please consider what you've read and learned, and journal your own personal response to this. This can be of great help in the future to see how you are progressing and changing.

5. Who is behind such responses?

2Corinthians 11:3 ~ But I am afraid that, as the serpent deceived Eve by his craftiness, your minds will be led astray from the simplicity and purity *of devotion* to Christ.

Every sinner is really the devil's drudge.

2Thessalonians 2:8-10 ~ [8] And then shall that Wicked be revealed, whom the Lord shall consume with the spirit of his mouth, and shall destroy with the brightness of his coming: [9] Even him, whose coming is after the working of Satan with all power and signs and lying wonders, [10] And with all deceivableness of unrighteousness in them that perish; because they received not the love of the truth, that they might be saved.

2Timothy 3:13 ~ [13] But evil men and seducers shall wax worse and worse, deceiving, and being deceived.

"Other slaves are forced against their will, but sinners are willing to be slaves, they will not take their freedom; they kiss their fetters." ~ Thomas Watson

Revelation 20:10 ~ And the devil that deceived them was cast into the lake of fire and brimstone, where the beast and the false prophet are, and shall be tormented day and night for ever and ever.

"It is so stupid of modern civilization to have given up believing in the devil when he is the only explanation of it." ~ R. Knox

If you despise Truth you fall in love with the lie!

At this time, please consider what you've read and learned, and journal your own personal response to this. This can be of great help in the future to see how you are progressing and changing.

6. What is the result of our abandoning the One, True Living GOD?

Jeremiah 2:19 ~ "Your own wickedness will correct you, and your apostasies will reprove you; Know therefore and see that it is evil and bitter for you to forsake the LORD your God, and the dread of Me is not in you," declares the Lord GOD of hosts.

The Bible teaches us that our struggle is not something that deserves the wrath of God; it is part of the wrath of God which rests on all of fallen humanity. He did not hold us back from the sin we desired, but allowed us to run into evil, that the pain it brought might move us to return to His outstretched arms.

"God whispers to us in our pleasures, speaks in our conscience, but shouts in our pains: it is HIS megaphone to rouse a deaf world." ~ C. S. Lewis

Romans 1:24 ~ Wherefore God also gave them up to uncleanness through the lusts of their own hearts, to dishonor their own bodies between themselves

Having lost touch with GOD Almighty, we lost ourselves. Many of us felt inadequate, unworthy, alone, and afraid. Early on, we came to feel disconnected--from parents, from peers, from ourselves. We tuned out with drugs, alcohol, promiscuity, [bad habits in general], fantasy, porn, and masturbation. We plugged in by drinking in the pictures, the images, and pursuing the objects of our fantasies. We lusted and wanted to be lusted after.

We became true addicts: sex with self (masturbation) & others, promiscuity, adultery, dependency relationships, and more, much much more.

We got it through the eyes; we bought it, we sold it, we traded it, we gave it away, some of us made it and distributed it. We were addicted to the intrigue, the tease and the forbidden.

The only way we know to be free of it was to do it. 'Please connect with me and make me whole!' we cried with out-stretched arms.

Lusting after the "big fix", we gave away our power to others. This produced guilt, self-hatred, remorse, emptiness, and pain, and we were driven ever inward, away from reality, away from love, lost inside ourselves.

Romans 1:26-27 ~ [26] For this cause God gave them up unto vile affections: for even their women did change the natural use into that which is against nature: [27] And likewise also the men, leaving the natural use of the woman, burned in their lust one toward another; men with men working that which is unseemly, and receiving in themselves that recompense of their error which was meet.

Many of us, who could understand GOD allowing us to follow our own desires only to draw us back to HIMSELF, were still troubled by the question, "Why did I have these desires in the first place?"

Some of us, having asked GOD for a miraculous release to no avail, and having struggled unsuccessfully against our feelings, came to the conclusion, "I am what I am and there's nothing I can do about it."

These thoughts challenged the ideas many of us had long tried to believe, and some of us found them frightening at first. As we reflected, however, we came to see that they were good news. They proved that we were not the prisoners of a cruel fate or faulty genes or hormones. Our problem was not physical and unchangeable but psychological and relational, and spiritual. There was hope for us! If we would draw near to GOD, work through our hurts, and establish healthy relationships, we could be free!

Much of what we call 'straight' is crooked by GOD'S definition. It isn't HIS plan to lead you out of one lust into another. The process of change involves an unlearning of the sinful, habitual condition, and then a learning of the GOD-Given identity in JESUS The CHRIST.

It is important to realize that much of what passes as normal is also fallen.

At this time, please consider what you've read and learned, and journal your own personal response to this. This can be of great help in the future to see how you are progressing and changing.

7. Could I have been deceived about my sexuality?

It is very important we understand the perversion of sexual-brokenness and the hold of it. Homosexuality is just one aspect of sexual-brokenness and of perversion. I would like us to replace the word "homosexuality" throughout this lesson with our own sexual sin, habit, stronghold. The sexual perversion distorts our GOD-Given Identity in JESUS

Proverbs 28:26 ~ He who trusts in his own heart is a fool, but he who walks wisely will be delivered.

So we must decide whether we will follow our feelings and our fears or take our stand on GOD'S Word, The Holy Bible!

Jeremiah 9:23-24 ~ [23] Thus saith the LORD, Let not the wise man glory in his wisdom, neither let the mighty man glory in his might, let not the rich man glory in his riches: [24] But let him that glorieth glory in this, that he understandeth and knoweth me, that I am the LORD which exercise lovingkindness, judgment, and righteousness, in the earth: for in these things I delight, saith the LORD.

Majority of the people who pride themselves on their knowledge or what they call 'wisdom', are simply boasting of educational ignorance.

1Corinthians 3:18-20 ~ [18] Let no man deceive himself. If any man among you seemeth to be wise in this world, let him become a fool, that he may be wise. [19] For the wisdom of this world is foolishness with God. For it is written, He taketh the wise in their own craftiness. [20] And again, The Lord knoweth the thoughts of the wise, that they are vain.

Ignorance is not bliss. Ignorance is bondage.

"I suppose that many might have attained to wisdom had they not thought they had already attained it." ~ An Exposition of Proverbs

"See your need of Christ's teaching. You cannot see your way without this morning star. The plumb line of reason is too short to fathom the deep things of God." ~ Thomas Watson

1Corinthians 8:2 ~ And if any man think that he knoweth anything, he knoweth nothing yet as he ought to know.

"The first step towards madness is to think oneself wise." ~ F. Rojas

Revelation 12:9 ~ And the great dragon was cast out, that old serpent, called the Devil, and Satan, which deceiveth the whole world: he was cast out into the earth, and his angels were cast out with him.

"Unbelief is the mother of sin, and misbelief the nurse of it." ~ Thomas Manton IV

At this time, please consider what you've read and learned, and journal your own personal response to this. This can be of great help in the future to see how you are progressing and changing.

8. What shall I do?

Jeremiah 3:22 ~ "Return, O faithless sons, I will heal your faithlessness. Behold, we come to You; For You are the LORD our God."

"His mercies are beyond all imagination; great mercies, manifold mercies, tender mercies, sure mercies, everlasting mercies; and all is yours, if you will but turn." ~ J. Alleine

Revelation 22:17 ~ And the Spirit and the bride say, Come. And let him that heareth say, Come. And let him that is athirst come. And whosoever will, let him take the water of life freely.

"Christ does not pull His sheep by a rope; in His army are none but volunteers." ~ E. Frommel

At this time, please consider what you've read and learned, and journal your own personal response to this. This can be of great help in the future to see how you are progressing and changing.

9. How important is Faith for me?

Ezekiel 33:11 ~ [11] Say to them, 'As I live!' declares the Lord GOD, 'I take no pleasure in the death of the wicked, but rather that the wicked turn from his way and live. Turn back, turn back from your evil ways! Why then will you die, O house of Israel?'

"The only reason people are going to hell is because all lifelong they have told GOD that they can live just fine without HIM. On the judgment day GOD will say, 'Based on your own decision to live life separately from ME, you will spend eternity separate from ME.' That's hell. GOD will not violate our will. If all lifelong we have said, 'my own will be done,' then on the day of judgment GOD will say to you, 'your will be done for eternity.'" ~ G. K. Chesterton

Hell is GOD'S great compliment to the reality of human freedom and the dignity of human choice. GOD doesn't send you to hell, but HE will honor your own choice to go there. Your own free will choice.

John 8:24 ~ [24] Therefore I said to you that you will die in your sins; for unless you believe that I am *He*, you will die in your sins."

Hebrews 11:6 ~ [6] And without faith it is impossible to please *Him*, for he who comes to God must believe that He is and *that* He is a rewarder of those who seek Him.

"As so much prominence is assigned to faith in the Scriptures, as all the promises of God are addressed to believers, and as all the conscious exercises of spiritual life involve the exercise of faith, without which they are impossible, the importance of this grace cannot be overestimated." ~ C. Hodge

At this time, please consider what you've read and learned, and journal your own personal response to this. This can be of great help in the future to see how you are progressing and changing.

10. What am I to believe in?

Psalm 18:2 ~ [2] The LORD is my rock and my fortress and my deliverer, my God, my rock, in whom I take refuge; My shield and the horn of my salvation, my stronghold.

Psalm 40:4 ~ [4] How blessed is the man who has made the LORD his trust, and has not turned to the proud, nor to those who lapse into falsehood.

J. H. Strong said, "Some years ago at a dinner party I found myself seated beside a brilliant young woman. There was a religious discussion, at the close of which she thought to sum matters up in these words: 'My guess is as good as your guess.' Well, I did not dispute it. I had no reason to be proud of my powers of guessing. For all I knew, her guess might be better than my guess. But her guess was not so good as my knowledge; and that I can say in all sincerity because I can recall a time when I sat exactly where she sat--guessing, speculating, balancing intellectual probabilities. I could have serene faith, so it seemed to me, if only questions were answered which weren't answered. But certitude is not getting one's questions answered. It is something different, something more. It does not come as the result and reward of a process of reasoning. It springs from a relationship."

Intimate relationships are what each one of us seeks, out of our very nature. That is a characteristic, or a desire, that we cannot change. What happens is that we misidentify it and then it all gets all confusing and fleshly.

John 14:6 ~ [6] Jesus said to him, "I am the way, and the truth, and the life; no one comes to the Father but through Me.

1John 5:9-12 ~ [9] If we receive the testimony of men, the testimony of God is greater; for the testimony of God is this, that He has testified concerning His Son. [10] The one who believes in the Son of God has the testimony in himself; the one who does not believe God has made Him a liar, because he has not believed in the testimony that God has given concerning His Son. [11] And the testimony is this, that God has given us eternal life, and this life is in His Son. [12] He who has the Son has the life; he who does not have the Son of God does not have the life.

At this time, please consider what you've read and learned, and journal your own personal response to this. This can be of great help in the future to see how you are progressing and changing.

11. Must there be some knowledge before there can be true Faith?

Romans 10:13-14 ~ [13] for "WHOEVER WILL CALL ON THE NAME OF THE LORD WILL BE SAVED." [14] How then will they call on Him in whom they have not believed? How will they believe in Him whom they have not heard? And how will they hear without a preacher?

"Faith need not be a hopeless leap into the dark. True biblical faith is a step into the light. In the light of God's Truth we can discover who we are, why we are here, and where we are going. We can encounter the fullness of life the Father has wanted for us all along." ~ R. S. Richards

"Scripture knowledge is the candle without which faith cannot see to do its work." ~ D. L. Moody

Romans 10:17 ~ [17] So faith *comes* from hearing, and hearing by the word of Christ.

"The Bible everywhere teaches that without knowledge there can be no faith. On this principle the Apostles acted everywhere. They went abroad preaching Christ, proving from the Scriptures that He was the Son of God and Savior of the world. The communication of knowledge always preceded the demand for faith." ~ C. Hodge

"Knowledge carries the torch of faith. True faith knows whom it believes, and why it believes. Faith is seated as well in the understanding as in the will. It has an eye to see Christ, as well as a wing to fly to him." ~ Thomas Watson

2Thessalonians 2:13-14 ~ [13] But we should always give thanks to God for you, brethren beloved by the Lord, because God has chosen you from the beginning for salvation through sanctification by the Spirit and faith in the truth. [14] It was for this He called you through our gospel, that you may gain the glory of our Lord Jesus Christ.

James tells us of two very distinct and separate wisdoms in James chapter 3, he tells of a wisdom from below and a wisdom from above.

Heavenly Wisdom or earthly wisdom.

At this time, please consider what you've read and learned, and journal your own personal response to this. This can be of great help in the future to see how you are progressing and changing.

12. What is Faith?

Psalm 36:7 ~ [7] How precious is Your lovingkindness, O God! And the children of men take refuge in the shadow of Your wings.

"Where can we rest our faith but upon God's faithfulness?"
Thomas Watson

Psalm 62:8 ~ [8] Trust in Him at all times, O people; Pour out your heart before Him; God is a refuge for us. *Selah.*

John 3:36 ~ [36] He who believes in the Son has eternal life; but he who does not obey the Son will not see life, but the wrath of God abides on him."

"Faith is knowledge passing into conviction, and it is conviction passing into confidence. Faith cannot stop short of self-commitment to Christ, a transference of reliance upon ourselves and all human resources to reliance upon Christ alone for salvation. Faith is not belief of propositions respecting the Savior, however essential an ingredient of faith such belief is. Faith is trust in a person, the person of Christ, the Son of God and Savior of the lost. It is entrustment of ourselves to Him. It is not simply believing Him; it is believing in Him and on Him." ~ J. Murray

"Faith means abandoning all trust in one's own resources. Faith means casting oneself unreservedly on the mercy of God. Faith means laying hold on the promises of God in Christ, relying entirely on the finished work of Christ for salvation, and on the power of the indwelling Holy Spirit of God for daily strength." ~ L. Morris

1 Timothy 6:17 ~ [17] Instruct those who are rich in this present world not to be conceited or to fix their hope on the uncertainty of riches, but on God, who richly supplies us with all things to enjoy.

At this time, please consider what you've read and learned, and journal your own personal response to this. This can be of great help in the future to see how you are progressing and changing.

13. How do I begin a life of Faith?

John 1:12 ~ [12] But as many as received Him, to them He gave the right to become children of God, *even* to those who believe in His name

The agnostic Gamaliel Bradford wrote, "The simple fact is, that, if God does not exist, the universe is but a wilderness of barren horror. If He does exist, life should be but one long effort to know Him and be at one with Him. Separation from Him is the most terrible punishment the mind can conceive."

Acts 2:21 ~ [21] 'AND IT SHALL BE THAT EVERYONE WHO CALLS ON THE NAME OF THE LORD WILL BE SAVED.'

Going into a church building doesn't make you a Christian any more than going into a garage makes you a car.

Revelation 3:20 ~ [20] Behold, I stand at the door and knock; if anyone hears My voice and opens the door, I will come in to him and will dine with him, and he with Me.

At this time, please consider what you've read and learned, and journal your own personal response to this. This can be of great help in the future to see how you are progressing and changing.

14. What attitude of heart comes with Faith?

Mark 1:14-15 ~ [14] Now after John had been taken into custody, Jesus came into Galilee, preaching the gospel of God, [15] and saying, "The time is fulfilled, and the kingdom of God is at hand; repent and believe in the gospel."

"Let no one imagine that he will lose anything of human dignity by this voluntary sell-out to his God. He does not by this degrade himself as a man; rather he finds his right place of high honor as one made in the image of his Creator. His deep disgrace lay in his moral derangement, his unnatural usurpation of the place of God. His honor will be proved by restoring again that stolen throne. In exalting God over all he finds his own highest honor upheld." ~ A. W. Tozer

Luke 13:5 ~ [5] I tell you, no, but unless you repent, you will all likewise perish.

"Man tried to set up on his own, to behave as if he belonged to himself. In other words, fallen man is not simply an imperfect creature who needs improvement: he is a rebel who must lay down his arms. Laying down your arms, surrendering, saying you are sorry, realizing that you have been on the wrong track and getting ready to start life over again from the ground floor--that is the only way out. This process of surrender --this movement full speed astern-- is what Christians call repentance. Now repentance is no fun at all. It means unlearning all the self-conceit and self-will that we have been training ourselves into for thousands of years. It means undergoing a kind of death. ~~~>

This repentance is not something God demands of you before He will take you back and which He could simply let you off if He chose: it is simply a description of what going back to Him is like. If you ask God to take you back without it, you are really asking Him to let you go back without going back. It cannot happen." ~ C. S. Lewis

Acts 3:19 ~ [19] Therefore repent and return, so that your sins may be wiped away, in order that times of refreshing may come from the presence of the Lord

"We should repent of what we have been, but rejoice in what we may be." ~ C. H. Spurgeon

Acts 17:30 ~ [30] Therefore having overlooked the times of ignorance, God is now declaring to men that all *people* everywhere should repent

Someone once said that GOD is always trying to give good things to us, but our hands are too full to receive them.

Some refuse to repent saying "we know ourselves too well to promise much to God!" That is bad theology. It is also bad spirituality. For God calls us to promise ourselves to Him in a lifelong commitment of faithfulness and obedience. He does not regard our failure as a becoming modesty, or an understandable reticence. He has other names for it: disobedience, disloyalty, faithlessness." ~ S. Ferguson

Acts 20:21 ~ [21] solemnly testifying to both Jews and Greeks of repentance toward God and faith in our Lord Jesus Christ. While it is true that the Faith with which we believe must be a repentant Faith, it is also true that the repentance with which we turn to JESUS The CHRIST must be a believing repentance. I read somewhere that even the tears of our repentance need to be washed in the Blood of CHRIST. The gospel calls men out of themselves and into HIM!

At this time, please consider what you've read and learned, and journal your own personal response to this. This can be of great help in the future to see how you are progressing and changing.

15. Why is it sometimes difficult to Believe?

John 3:18-21 ~ [18] He who believes in Him is not judged; he who does not believe has been judged already, because he has not believed in the name of the only begotten Son of God. [19] This is the judgment, that the Light has come into the world, and men loved the darkness rather than the Light, for their deeds were evil. [20] For everyone who does evil hates the Light, and does not come to the Light for fear that his deeds will be exposed. [21] But he who practices the truth comes to the Light, so that his deeds may be manifested as having been wrought in God."

Unbelievers have sometimes been quite candid about the reasons for their unbelief.

"I had motives for not wanting the world to have a meaning; consequently, assumed that it had none, and was able without any difficulty to find satisfying reasons for this assumption. The philosopher who finds no meaning in the world is not concerned exclusively with a problem in pure metaphysics, he is also concerned to prove that there is no valid reason why he personally should not do as he wants to do. For myself, the philosophy of meaninglessness was essentially an instrument of liberation, sexual and political." ~ A. Huxley

"Choose well! Your choice is brief, yet endless." ~ A W Blackwood

John 5:44 ~ [44] How can you believe, when you receive glory from one another and you do not seek the glory that is from the *one and* only God?

One of the famous questions of the deceived is, 'If Christianity is true, why do the majority of intelligent people not believe it?'

The answer is simple, it is the same as the reason the majority of unintelligent people don't believe it. They don't want to have to accept the moral demands it would make on their lives.

John 7:16-17 ~ [16] So Jesus answered them and said, "My teaching is not Mine, but His who sent Me. [17] If anyone is willing to do His will, he will know of the teaching, whether it is of God or *whether* I speak from Myself.

"The Christian ideal has not been tried and found wanting. It has been found difficult and left untried." ~ G. K. Chesterton

Hebrews 3:12 ~ [12] Take care, brethren, that there not be in any one of you an evil, unbelieving heart that falls away from the living God.

At this time, please consider what you've read and learned, and journal your own personal response to this. This can be of great help in the future to see how you are progressing and changing.

16. Will I need GOD'S help to believe?

John 6:44 ~ [44] No one can come to Me unless the Father who sent Me draws him; and I will raise him up on the last day.

There are several Truths taught in the Bible that we must remember as we consider this verse. We must never suppose that the doctrine of this verse takes away man's responsibility and accountableness to GOD for his soul. On the contrary, the Bible always distinctly declares that if any man is lost, it is his own fault, he 'loses his own soul.' (Mark 8:36.)

We must not allow the doctrine of this verse to make us limit or narrow the offer of the hope of eternal salvation that is available to each one of us. On the contrary, we must hold firmly that pardon and peace are to be offered freely through JESUS The CHRIST to every man and woman without exception. We never know who they are that GOD will draw. Our duty is two-fold, evangelize and disciple.

We must not suppose that we, or anybody else, are drawn, unless we come to JESUS The CHRIST by Faith. This is the grand mark and evidence of any one being the subject of The FATHER'S drawing work.

We must always remember that GOD Almighty ordinarily works by means, and especially by such means as HE HIMSELF has appointed. We cannot pretend to explain why some are drawn and others do not heed the 'drawing' process.

"Until the Father draws the heart of man by His grace, man will not believe. His inability is not physical, but moral. It would not be true to say that a man has a real desire to come to Christ, but no power to come. It would be far more true to say that a man has no power to come because he has no desire or wish. It is not true that he would come if he could. It is true that he could come if he would. The corrupt will, the secret disinclination, the want of heart, are the real causes of unbelief. The power that we want is a new will. It is precisely at this point that we need the 'drawing' of the Father." ~ J. C. Ryle

1Corinthians 2:14 ~ [14] But a natural man does not accept the things of the Spirit of God, for they are foolishness to him; and he cannot understand them, because they are spiritually appraised

"You might as well try to describe a sunset to a blind man, play music to a deaf man, and talk to a dead man, as to discuss the deep things of God with an unconverted sinner. We might as well try to catch sunbeams with a fishhook or talk nuclear physics with a monument in a city park. The most erudite Ph.D. cannot take it in any better than a hillbilly; it is casting pearls before swine. As far as spiritual realities are concerned, a man who has not been born again is blind and can't see, deaf and can't hear, dead and can't feel." ~ V. Havner

2Corinthians 4:3-6 ~ [3] And even if our gospel is veiled, it is veiled to those who are perishing, [4] in whose case the god of this world has blinded the minds of the unbelieving so that they might not see the light of the gospel of the glory of Christ, who is the image of God. ~~~>

[5] For we do not preach ourselves but Christ Jesus as Lord, and ourselves as your bond-servants for Jesus' sake. [6] For God, who said, "Light shall shine out of darkness," is the One who has shone in our hearts to give the Light of the knowledge of the glory of God in the face of Christ.

"God pours the golden oil of mercy into empty vessels." ~ Thomas Watson

At this time, please consider what you've read and learned, and journal your own personal response to this. This can be of great help in the future to see how you are progressing and changing.

17. Should Faith be a daily attitude of heart?

John 8:31 ~ [31] So Jesus was saying to those Jews who had believed Him, "If you continue in My word, *then* you are truly disciples of Mine

"Relying on God has to begin all over again every day as if nothing had yet been done." ~ C. S. Lewis

"The promise of a kingdom", says Chrysostom, "is not made to them that heard Christ or followed Him, but that continued with Him."

Colossians 2:6-8 ~ [6] Therefore as you have received Christ Jesus the Lord, *so* walk in Him, [7] having been firmly rooted *and now* being built up in Him and established in your faith, just as you were instructed, *and* overflowing with gratitude.

[8] See to it that no one takes you captive through philosophy and empty deception, according to the tradition of men, according to the elementary principles of the world, rather than according to Christ.

Hebrews 10:35-36 ~ [35] Therefore, do not throw away your confidence, which has a great reward. [36] For you have need of endurance, so that when you have done the will of God, you may receive what was promised.

It is so easy, even after having made a commitment, to stop trusting The FATHER at some point. We can do so almost without realizing what is happening.

Old habits reassert themselves and suddenly we find ourselves trying to follow our own ideas instead of GOD'S Word, trying to work out our own solutions instead of trusting and obeying HIS Plan, trying to realize our own desires instead of HIS Will.

When we discover this, we may get discouraged and be tempted to give up. Just remember, GOD Almighty will joyously forgive (HE will abundantly pardon/Isaiah 55:7) us the moment we turn back to HIM and HE will again begin to give us the Freedom we seek.

At this time, please consider what you've read and learned, and journal your own personal response to this. This can be of great help in the future to see how you are progressing and changing.

18. Will true Faith change my life?

2 Chronicles 20:20 ~ [20] They rose early in the morning and went out to the wilderness of Tekoa; and when they went out, Jehoshaphat stood and said, "Listen to me, O Judah and inhabitants of Jerusalem, put your trust in the LORD your God and you will be established. Put your trust in His prophets and succeed."

Psalm 84:12 ~ O LORD of hosts, how blessed is the man who trusts in You!

"Every man carries his kingdom within, and no one knows what is taking place in another's kingdom. 'No one understands me!' Of course they don't, each one of us is a mystery. There is only One Who understands you, and that is God. Hand yourself over to Him." ~ O. Chambers

Psalm 125:1 ~ Those who trust in the LORD are as Mount Zion, which cannot be moved but abides forever.

"Faith melts our will into the will of God. It not only believes the promise, but obeys the command." ~ Thomas Watson

Romans 5:1-3 ~ [1] Therefore, having been justified by faith, we have peace with God through our Lord Jesus Christ, [2] through whom also we have obtained our introduction by faith into this grace in which we stand; and we exult in hope of the glory of God. [3] And not only this, but we also exult in our tribulations, knowing that tribulation brings about perseverance

"Holiness is constant agreement with God." ~ T. L. Cuyler

Galatians 5:6 ~ ⁶ For in Christ Jesus neither circumcision nor uncircumcision means anything, but faith working through love.

"Nothing matters but this: does Jesus have the utter absolute first and final say in your life?" ~ V. Havner

James 2:26 ~ ²⁶ For just as the body without *the* spirit is dead, so also faith without works is dead.

All temptation that comes our way is meant to take our eyes off The LORD and to take account of our own appearances. Faith is always meeting a mountain, a mountain of contradiction in the realm of tangible fact--of failures in deed, as well as in the realm of thoughts and feelings--and either faith or the mountain must go. They cannot both stand.

The trouble is that many times the mountain stays and Faith goes. This must not be.

If we resort to our senses to discover the Truth, we shall find the devil's lies are often enough true in our experience; but if we refuse to accept anything that contradicts GOD'S Word and maintain our Faith in HIM alone, we shall find that the devil's lies begin to dissolve and that our experience is coming progressively to account with that Word.

Hebrews 11:8 ~ [8] By faith Abraham, when he was called, obeyed by going out to a place which he was to receive for an inheritance; and he went out, not knowing where he was going.

At this time, please consider what you've read and learned, and journal your own personal response to this. This can be of great help in the future to see how you are progressing and changing.

19. Will Faith give me strength for my struggle?

Matthew 9:28-29 ~ [28] When He entered the house, the blind men came up to Him, and Jesus *said to them, "Do you believe that I am able to do this?" They *said to Him, "Yes, Lord." [29] Then He touched their eyes, saying, "It shall be done to you according to your faith."

Faith can also open our eyes to things we have not seen before, making us very aware of what we have missed, denied, been blinded to, or just ignored.

With my own experience as a former homosexual/transgender, I have come to realize many things, one being that as individuals are introduced to homosexuality, they automatically, without even consideration, accept the labels of that world. Putting on that identity which closes many other doors and draws lines that would not otherwise exist.

I was labeled a homosexual/transgender, and I accepted that without ever considering it as anything but "normal". Everything that occurred in my life after that one deceptive acceptance of that identity happened to a homosexual or a transgender person in my thoughts and feelings, in my own reasoning.

Any of the characteristics or desires of heterosexuality, or just from me being a male, were totally silenced and denied automatically without me ever having to consider or recognize them. This was due to my own delusion of my thoughts and feelings based on an, or some, experience/s.

My brain was trained to deny anything outside of my emotional and mental state of belief. I was deceived from a very early age. Lack of intimacy, lack of Truth and lack of knowledge.

Once a person believes that they are something very specific, it is almost impossible to make them believe something different because it goes against their thoughts and feelings. This was not just something I did, it was who and what I was!

It is almost like when we do have natural, or normal, sexual urges or attractions that those are immediately denied and blocked out because of the lie that we have already accepted.

For me, I could not possibly be attracted to the opposite sex because I had accepted, and put on, the identity of a homosexual and a transgender person. Which is why homosexuality is not 'just another sin'.

I was blinded to everything around me that was not in line with my own thoughts & feelings, my deception. This deception distorted my entire perception of everything that was going on around me as well as within me! For me, any male was a potential sex partner and could give me "love" and the "affirmation" I was seeking.

My reality was distorted. My reality was not reality at all but a fantasy land of emotional turmoil and desire for attention. This had to be corrected by Faith.

Faith allows us to see things through GOD'S lens and to recognize our good, and unchangeable heterosexual design. Faith gives sight!

As we, through Faith in GOD'S Word, reject the lie that "we are homosexual, transgender or gender-fluid, and cannot change", and embrace the Truth that we are heterosexual by design, by Creation, by Intent and in JESUS The CHRIST our identity abides, then reality can be clearly seen and healing can begin.

Mark 9:23 ~ 23 And Jesus said to him, "'If You can?' All things are possible to him who believes."

It is most times our own doubts that keep us from acting and overcoming. Accepting the identity of homosexual is much different than just engaging in the sin of homosexuality. There are some very clear distinctions we will discuss as we continue further.

I was a part of the lgbt community. I had "put on" that identity. However, many of the men that engaged in homosexuality with me were not a part of the lgbt community and had not "put on" that identity. They simply were satisfying the lusts of their flesh. Big difference.

Just like JESUS said, in Mark 9:23, that "all things are possible to him who believe", the same is true for unbelief. We become our own worst enemy by not believing Truth and believing a lie. That lie traps us, and we are caught up in the web of deception against our own selves and only JESUS The CHRIST can rescue us as we hang on that cliff clenching those rocks.

Faith is what we gain, and what grows as we surrender and trust The FATHER.

"Our Lord did not rebuke His disciples for making mistakes, but for not having Faith." ~ O. Chambers

Ephesians 6:16 ~ [16] in addition to all, taking up the shield of faith with which you will be able to extinguish all the flaming arrows of the evil *one.*

Psychologist Will James said, "The greatest revolution of our generation is the discovery that human beings, by changing the inner attitudes of their minds, can change the outer aspects of their lives."

Hebrews 11:32-34 ~ [32] And what more shall I say? For time will fail me if I tell of Gideon, Barak, Samson, Jephthah, of David and Samuel and the prophets, [33] who by faith conquered kingdoms, performed *acts of* righteousness, obtained promises, shut the mouths of lions, [34] quenched the power of fire, escaped the edge of the sword, from weakness were made strong, became mighty in war, put foreign armies to flight.

"Far better it is to dare mighty things, to win glorious triumphs, even though checkered by failure, than to take rank with those poor spirits who neither enjoy much nor suffer much, because they live in the gray twilight that knows not victory nor defeat." ~ T. Roosevelt

1John 5:4 ~ [4] For whatever is born of God overcomes the world; and this is the victory that has overcome the world — our faith.

"Press on! Nothing in the world can take the place of perseverance. Talent will not; nothing is more common than unsuccessful men with talent. Genius will not; unrewarded genius is almost a proverb. Education will not; the world is full of educated derelicts. Persistence and determination alone are omnipotent." ~ C. Coolidge

So, when you hurt and are tempted to give up, walk by Faith in the promises of YAHWEH, GOD Almighty.

When you find yourself thinking of turning aside, remember that to do so is only to postpone the process of your discovery and to make the process ultimately more difficult and painful.

Feel your pain, deal with it by Faith in the promises of GOD and press on to the Freedom that HE has promised.

Galatians 6:9 ~ [9] Let us not lose heart in doing good, for in due time we will reap if we do not grow weary.

I read a prayer once that went like this, "God of our life, there are days when the burdens we carry chafe our shoulders and weigh us down; when the road seems dreary and endless, the skies grey and threatening; when our lives have no music in them, and our hearts are lonely, and our souls have lost their courage.

Flood the path with light, we beseech Thee; turn our eyes to where the skies are full of promise; tune our hearts to brave music; give us the sense of comradeship with heroes and saints of every age; and so quicken our spirits that we may be able to encourage the souls of all who journey with us on the road of life, to Thy honor and glory."

Hebrews 11:24-26 ~ [24] By faith Moses, when he had grown up, refused to be called the son of Pharaoh's daughter, [25] choosing rather to endure ill-treatment with the people of God than to enjoy the passing pleasures of sin, [26] considering the reproach of Christ greater riches than the treasures of Egypt; for he was looking to the reward.

It seems easier for us to blame others for our grief or misery rather than to take the necessary steps to deal with it and get over it, making ourselves feel better.

"We even talk about our own feelings as if they were visitors from outer space. We say, 'This feeling came over me,' as if we were helpless creatures overwhelmed by mysterious forces, instead of simply saying, 'I felt that way.' We speak as if our feelings change from sunny to stormy like the weather, over which we have no control. This meteorological view of our emotions is very useful; it takes us off the hook for the way we feel. We diminish ourselves, just in order to push away the chance of choice." ~ M. Newman

"Faith is simply the bringing of our minds into accord with the truth. It is adjusting our expectations to the promises of God in complete assurance that the God of the whole earth cannot lie." ~ A. W. Tozer

There is an old folklore which says that GOD saw that the devil had too many weapons in his armory and decided that they should be drastically reduced. The devil was allowed to choose only one of all his weapons with which to try to maintain his power. Satan decided to keep discouragement as his one weapon because, he said, "If only I can persuade men and women to be thoroughly discouraged, they will make no further moral effort, and then I shall be enthroned in their lives."

Joshua 1:9 ~ [9] Have I not commanded you? Be strong and courageous! Do not tremble or be dismayed, for the LORD your God is with you wherever you go.

At this time, please consider what you've read and learned, and journal your own personal response to this. This can be of great help in the future to see how you are progressing and changing.

20. Must my Faith be perfect for GOD to Bless it?

Matthew 14:25-31 ~ [25] And in the fourth watch of the night He came to them, walking on the sea. [26] When the disciples saw Him walking on the sea, they were terrified, and said, "It is a ghost!" And they cried out in fear. [27] But immediately Jesus spoke to them, saying, "Take courage, it is I; do not be afraid."

[28] Peter said to Him, "Lord, if it is You, command me to come to You on the water." [29] And He said, "Come!" And Peter got out of the boat, and walked on the water and came toward Jesus. [30] But seeing the wind, he became frightened, and beginning to sink, he cried out, "Lord, save me!" [31] Immediately Jesus stretched out His hand and took hold of him, and *said to him, "You of little faith, why did you doubt?"

The power of Faith isn't in itself. Faith is not something that merits the favor of GOD. All the effectiveness for the hope of eternal salvation is in JESUS The CHRIST. The true character of Faith looks away from itself.

Matthew 17:20 ~ [20] And He said to them, "Because of the littleness of your faith; for truly I say to you, if you have faith the size of a mustard seed, you will say to this mountain, 'Move from here to there,' and it will move; and nothing will be impossible to you. He

178

Mark 9:24 ~ 24 Immediately the boy's father cried out and said, "I do believe; help my unbelief."

At this time, please consider what you've read and learned, and journal your own personal response to this. This can be of great help in the future to see how you are progressing and changing.

21. Will my Faith be tested?

Genesis 22:1-2 ~ 1 Now it came about after these things, that God tested Abraham, and said to him, "Abraham!" And he said, "Here I am." 2 He said, "Take now your son, your only son, whom you love, Isaac, and go to the land of Moriah, and offer him there as a burnt offering on one of the mountains of which I will tell you."

"Why is temptation so attractive, unrelenting, and powerful? Surely God could make it easier for us. I'm not saying that God causes us to sin; nor does He tempt us as Satan does. But God does test us; He also allows Satan to tempt us. Why? Temptation, with all of its frightful possibilities for failure, is God's method of testing our loyalties. We cannot say that we love someone until we have had to make some hard choices on his behalf. Similarly, we cannot say we love God unless we've said NO to persistent temptations. God is allowing us the luxury of difficult choices so that we can prove our love for Him. These are our opportunities to choose God rather than the world." ~ E. M. Lutzer

Deuteronomy 8:2 ~ 2 You shall remember all the way which the LORD your God has led you in the wilderness these forty years, that He might humble you, testing you, to know what was in your heart, whether you would keep His commandments or not.

Proverbs 17:3 ~ 3 The refining pot is for silver and the furnace for gold, but the LORD tests hearts.

"Being a Christian means joy, peace, and contentment, we are told. We happily misconstrue that to mean a Christian never has problems or pain. We'll be protected by our all-powerful Bodyguard from losing our jobs, suffering from illness, or having accidents because that all happens to 'other' people. We want to believe it, so we do. This one lie may be the most insidious religious falsehood in Christendom. It becomes a source of bitterness and anger the moment life turns sour. God often becomes the scapegoat for all the hurt we feel when He doesn't come charging to the rescue. The truth is that life is difficult. Faith makes it less difficult, not by solving the problems through rescue, but by giving us a resource to handle the problems." ~ C. Thurman

Hebrews 11:17-19 ~ 17 By faith Abraham, when he was tested, offered up Isaac, and he who had received the promises was offering up his only begotten *son*; 18 *it was he* to whom it was said, "IN ISAAC YOUR DESCENDANTS SHALL BE CALLED." 19 He considered that God is able to raise *people* even from the dead, from which he also received him back as a type.

1Peter 1:7 ~ 7 so that the proof of your faith, *being* more precious than gold which is perishable, even though tested by fire, may be found to result in praise and glory and honor at the revelation of Jesus Christ

When we feel helpless we can praise GOD that HE helps the helpless! When we feel ungodly we can praise GOD that HE Loved us so much that HE robed HIMSELF in flesh, came to this Earth, to become The Man JESUS CHRIST, to die for our sin! When we feel anxious we can praise GOD that HE brings good out of trouble!

When we are tempted we can praise GOD that HE has broken the power of the bondage that once had a hold on each one of us!

When we feel confused about our identity we can praise GOD that HE has Created us, intended for us to be, and Designed our identity intimately intertwined in JESUS The CHRIST!

Ephesians 5:18-20 ~ [18] And do not get drunk with wine, for that is dissipation, but be filled with the Spirit, [19] speaking to one another in psalms and hymns and spiritual songs, singing and making melody with your heart to the Lord; [20] always giving thanks for all things in the name of our Lord Jesus Christ to God, even the Father

At this time, please consider what you've read and learned, and journal your own personal response to this. This can be of great help in the future to see how you are progressing and changing.

Purpose 3. To be able to Trust our FATHER in Heaven, confident that it will bring us into a familiar and familial bond with HIM, and our brethren (brothers & sisters). Intimacy!

Trusting GOD Almighty as HE reveals our true identity is a really big step for many of us because trust doesn't come easy for us. We must trust HIM, confident and focused on the fact that it will bring us into a familiar and familial bond with HIM, and others. Intimacy!

Know this; neither the liberal nor conservative views regarding sin serves the healing purposes of GOD Almighty. I am not a democrat. I am not a republican. I am a Man of GOD and as a man of GOD I must see things through GOD'S lens. I am liberal on some issues and conservative on other issues. We must stay focused on the commission already given us and not look to men and their weak understanding or personal interpretation of The Word. So, let's focus on us and those around us.

In spite of our own helplessness and emotional turmoil, there is Freedom found in JESUS The CHRIST, and HE accepts us. HE has broken the power of our strongholds, our habits, our addictions, our sins, at the cross. Yet that doesn't mean we have nothing else to do.

Created in the image of YAHWEH, GOD Almighty; born in the image of Adam.

While sin has distorted HIS Image in us, our One True Living GOD robed HIMSELF in flesh, came to this earth becoming the man, YESHUA, JESUS The CHRIST, to be the sacrifice for your wrongs and mine! HE suffered death to Redeem us from all iniquity and to restore us to our intended identity, and to restore us in the liberty HE desires for HIS Children. We have solid Hope!

To enter into all of this, we must continue to press forward towards the mark. Will we entrust our lives into those hands that were pierced for us? Will we commit ourselves to doing HIS Will rather than our own? Are we ready to trust HIS Guidance rather than our own, or others', ideas of what is best for us?

Our lives have been "unmanageable," we must know by now that they have been under the wrong management. Now it is time that we learn how to give our life over to the Only ONE who can properly manage it.

We may have tried to entrust our lives to HIM before and failed. We may have entrusted our lives to HIM at one time and taken them back.

Whatever may have gone wrong before, now we seek what HE desires for us, to rediscover who HE Created us to be in JESUS CHRIST.

At one time I managed to confuse knowledge with faith. I thought that the more Bible I crammed into my head, the more Faith I would have. I studied the Bible morning by morning, faithfully attended Sunday School and "church" and entered the ministry. I filled my head with Bible truth only to find that my Faith was still not strong enough to withstand the blows that came to me in life.

Please do not misunderstand. Knowledge is necessary. You cannot trust in The One you do not know. Knowledge alone, however, is not enough for Faith. "Faith cometh by hearing, and hearing by the word of GOD" (Romans 10:17), but faith is not merely hearing. It only comes by hearing.

Knowledge is the beginning of faith, but it is only the beginning. Truth must filter down from our heads into the very fiber of our souls. This does not happen quickly or easily. It is not obtained by mere human effort. It is the gift of GOD over time. I learned this slowly and painfully. And guess what? I am still learning, and will continue to 'be learning' until HE comes for me.

In the past, before surrendering to YESHUA, JESUS The CHRIST, when life overwhelmed me, I turned for comfort to homosexual activity, pornography, masturbation, gambling, drugs, and the list goes on. This only led to greater woe--guilt, shame, fear, prison, disease, hurt, the loss of family and friends.

In the first few years of my walk there was doubt that I had any faith at all. I constantly feared that I could be lost forever--that JESUS would abandon me, and that HIS final word to me would be, " 'I never knew you; DEPART FROM ME, YOU WHO PRACTICE LAWLESSNESS.'" (Matthew 7:21-23).

And then, at a very low point in my walk, after I stumbled big time, GOD HIMSELF reached out to me. I cannot explain or describe it. Words are inadequate. But HE took the Truths I had learned (that study was not in vain!) and began to apply them to my heart. Tenderly, The HOLY SPIRIT applied the balm of HIS Truth to my soul, and slowly I began to revive.

HE gave me a heart transplant.

Not only did YAHWEH minister to my heart directly, HE also used others to open my eyes to the meaning of HIS Scriptures for my life. HE taught me to meditate on HIS Truth until I could see how it applied to me and then to praise HIM for the mercy and grace I experienced as a result of this process.

Please be assured I still have much to learn.

I agree with the Apostle Paul, "[12] Not that I have already obtained *it* or have already become perfect, but I press on so that I may lay hold of that for which also I was laid hold of by Christ Jesus. [13] Brethren, I do not regard myself as having laid hold of *it* yet; but one thing *I do*: forgetting what *lies* behind and reaching forward to what *lies* ahead, [14] I press on toward the goal for the prize of the upward call of God in Christ Jesus." ~ Philippians 3:12-14

Helpful Hints

1) Read your Bible each morning until you find a verse which speaks to your situation. Write it on an index card and carry it with you throughout the day for meditation. As you ask GOD to show you what this word from HIM means for your life, jot the thoughts that come to you on the back of the card. Prayerfully write these thoughts out more fully in your journal and conclude with a written prayer of thanksgiving to GOD for what this Truth means to you. Share some of these thoughts.

2) Write an account of how you came to believe the lie and how there was nothing you could do about it in your journal. What have you done and what are you doing to escape it? What progress have you made?

3) Memorize one of the verses you found helpful in this chapter.

Believing the lie was, for me, a process. Recognizing and renouncing the lie is also a process. Illusions do not die easily! Through reading The Bible, I began to understand the why of this struggle. The lie draws its strength from confusion, but light dispels darkness and truth destroys error. As I learned that this was not a physical problem, but a spiritual one, it was then that my faith grew stronger.

Method 4. Create an extremely transparent and very humbling moral inventory.

Purpose 4. We write down this moral and very convicting inventory to reveal to us exactly who and what we are and had become. We utilize this inventory in Method 5

We who seek Freedom from bondage, strongholds, habits, addictions, sins, etc... will fall short of our goal if we do not work each of these methods in the order of which they are. This is not earthly wisdom, but Heavenly.

Some of us make the mistake of working only the relational side. In doing so, we run the risk of looking to man to meet needs that only The FATHER can satisfy. Human beings are limited, and we cannot always be available to one another and sometimes we do not even know how to help.

Most importantly, we are fallen creatures who can fail ourselves and others terribly. When this happens to one who has not learned to look to The FATHER for wisdom, comfort, and strength; then old emotional wounds can be opened and even magnified. So, the person who fails to work the spiritual side of these steps as well, hinders his or her own progress also.

Let's not forget that YAHWEH, GOD Almighty, said that it was not good for man to be alone (Genesis 2:18). GOD made this astounding statement before the fall, while Adam was enjoying perfect fellowship with HIM in the garden. It was not enough.

Man needed a helper like himself. Adam had no wounds from childhood that needed healing. Those who struggle may not yet be ready for relationships, or even marriage, but the Bible does stress the importance of fellowship and kinship, of establishing intimate same-sex relationships.

GOD has ordained that HE will meet some needs only through another human being. HE will heal some wounds only through other people. So, the person who fails to work the relational and the spiritual side of these methods hinders his or her own progress.

Be fearless and very thorough from the beginning. To begin the relational side of our discovery, we must do that one thing that we have always avoided and even dreaded. We must face ourselves and discover those defects of character which have poisoned our past lives, relationships, outlooks, etc....

The longer we put this off, the more we will find ourselves using drugs, alcohol, sex (whether with others, in our minds, or with ourselves), gambling, obsessions, and many other vices and strongholds, to deaden our feelings of shame, fear, and isolation.

Such responses only increase the feeling that we are filthy, guilty, and worthless, which produces greater desires to escape into darkness to punish or comfort ourselves. We must begin our extremely transparent and very humbling moral inventory fearlessly so that we can see clearly how to break free from the forces which have kept us in bondage.

1. What Truth must I clearly understand before I can make my extremely transparent and very humbling moral inventory because it is very difficult to face my failures and deepest & darkest secrets?

Psalm 86:5 ~ [5] For You, Lord, are good, and ready to forgive, and abundant in lovingkindness to all who call upon You.

Psalm 103:12 ~ [12] As far as the east is from the west, so far has He removed our transgressions from us.

These two, east & west, can never be brought together and so it is with our sins and us when forgiven. Once we are washed clean of our sin, it is gone forever.

Not saying that we cannot put on some new sin, just that our old sins are washed away for good!

Acts 13:38-39 ~ [38] Therefore let it be known to you, brethren, that through Him forgiveness of sins is proclaimed to you, [39] and through Him everyone who believes is freed from all things, from which you could not be freed through the Law of Moses.

Romans 8:1 ~ Therefore there is now no condemnation for those who are in Christ Jesus.

Romans 8:33-34 ~ [33] Who will bring a charge against God's elect? God is the one who justifies; [34] who is the one who condemns? Christ Jesus is He who died, yes, rather who was raised, who is at the right hand of God, who also intercedes for us.

It is condemnation that brings the sinners heart to repentance.

While some will not face their failures because they are proudly stubborn, others cannot do so because they are self-deceived. I was sincerely doing what I truly thought & felt to be right (in my own eyes). Although I may have always known "something wasn't quite right", I did not know I was living in sin or was going against GOD'S very intent for my entire identity.

I had no clue that I had "put on" a false identity. I had no idea that I misidentified my GOD-Given desire for same-sex intimacy with a non-existent "same-sex attraction" that ultimately led me to have same-sex desires sexually.

I was chatting once with a man who contacted me because of his desire, or lusts, to molest a child. He was a victim, and he finally saw The Light while reading The Scriptures one day. He clearly saw that when he was victimized it stopped something in him mentally and emotionally.

He felt/found comfort in engaging in sexual activity with men and boys as a child, and so that same self-deceived process carried into his adult years. This is a fact for so many out there.

It was only once he discovered what a true Intimate relationship was that he found Freedom from those lusts and desires.

Jeremiah 17:9 ~ 9 "The heart is more deceitful than all else and is desperately sick; Who can understand it?

Denial is one way all of us deceive ourselves. We keep ourselves from facing reality and lock ourselves into increasingly destructive patterns of behavior by;

<u>Outright Denial</u>: refusing to acknowledge an existing problem to ourselves and/or others.

<u>Minimizing</u>: acknowledging the problem but refusing to face its severity.

<u>Rationalizing</u>: acknowledging the problem but offering excuses to justify it.

<u>Dodging</u>: changing the subject when the conversation begins to deal with the problem.

<u>Attacking</u>: getting angry when the problem is discussed, thus avoiding the real issue.

<u>Blaming</u>: acknowledging the problem but refusing to take responsibility for current behavior by saying it is someone else's fault.

If you recognize any of these tendencies in yourself, put them to death right now if you really ever want Freedom from the strongholds, the habits, the addictions, and any sinful way that you may be indulging in.

We can also deceive ourselves by taking other people's inventories instead of our own. We cannot change them; we must be focused on changing our own patterns, and our own thoughts and feelings!

Matthew 7:3-5 ~ [3] Why do you look at the speck that is in your brother's eye, but do not notice the log that is in your own eye? [4] Or how can you say to your brother, 'Let me take the speck out of your eye,' and behold, the log is in your own eye? [5] You hypocrite, first take the log out of your own eye, and then you will see clearly to take the speck out of your brother's eye.

You see, we are called to judge what is right and what is wrong, and to do so Righteously. JESUS The CHRIST said to judge. But know that there is a difference between judging and passing judgment.

Pride can take the form of perfectionism which blinds us to our own faults and makes us quick to see the failings of others.

James 4:6 ~ [6] But He gives a greater grace. Therefore *it* says, "GOD IS OPPOSED TO THE PROUD, BUT GIVES GRACE TO THE HUMBLE."

I once read that Moroccans make rugs with deliberate imperfections. Designs are purposely woven with 'mistakes' in the pattern. Rug makers believe it is either ludicrous or blasphemous to attempt perfection when only GOD is perfect, and flaws are seen as reminders that humans are only human.

At this time, please consider what you've read and learned, and journal your own personal response to this. This can be of great help in the future to see how you are progressing and changing.

2. Why is it important for me to face myself?

Psalm 32:3-5 ~ ³ When I kept silent *about my sin*, my body wasted away through my groaning all day long. ⁴ For day and night Your hand was heavy upon me; My vitality was drained away *as* with the fever heat of summer. *Selah.*

⁵ I acknowledged my sin to You, and my iniquity I did not hide; I said, "I will confess my transgressions to the LORD"; And You forgave the guilt of my sin. *Selah.*

Who would not declare all his debts if they were certain to be paid in full by another? Seriously!

"Sin is a serpent, and he that covers sin does but keep it warm, that it may sting them more fiercely." ~ J. Donne

The majority of our interaction with other people is controlled by our own response to, ignorance, old hurts and traumatic experiences from our childhood.

It is so very important that each of us become connected with those old feelings and experience those old wounds in order for them to be healed.

If we don't, they will be that 'residue' that eventually permeates our skin and draws us back into the darkness of secrets, lies, guilt and shame. Nothing can get better on its own.

Time doesn't heal all wounds, it only allows the hurt to embed itself deeper, the resentment to strangle us, and for our daily lives to become more and more difficult.

Psalm 51:6 ~ 6 Behold, You desire truth in the innermost being, and in the hidden part You will make me know wisdom.

"There is no greater disaster in the spiritual life than to be immersed in unreality." ~ T. M.

"I remember approaching the office of a Christian mission and was puzzled to hear bangs and clatters and voices lifted up in anger--this was a Christian office! Two colleagues were physically wrestling over a telephone headset. When I attempted to arbitrate, it was fascinating to hear both of them protesting that they had nothing against the other. This was obviously not true; wrestling the phone from one another was a symptom of a real problem, one they weren't prepared to confess. Until they did so, there was no possibility for trust, restoration and spiritual harmony." ~ A. Dixson

Psalm 81:10-16 ~ 10 "I, the LORD, am your God, Who brought you up from the land of Egypt; Open your mouth wide and I will fill it. 11 "But My people did not listen to My voice, and Israel did not obey Me.

12 "So I gave them over to the stubbornness of their heart, to walk in their own devices. 13 "Oh that My people would listen to Me, that Israel would walk in My ways! 14 "I would quickly subdue their enemies and turn My hand against their adversaries

15 "Those who hate the LORD would pretend obedience to Him, and their time *of punishment* would be forever. 16 "But I would feed you with the finest of the wheat, and with honey from the rock I would satisfy you."

One vital barrier against falling back into our old, destructive patterns is a clear record of the pain our old sinful lives involved. If we can only remember what that sinful life cost us, we will do whatever it takes to avoid a return to that terrible misery.

"The burnt child dreads the fire" as long as he can recollect the pain! So, our extremely transparent and very humbling moral inventory is an essential link in our discovery of who, and what, we were Created to be in JESUS The CHRIST.

Galatians 6:7-8 ~ [7] Do not be deceived, God is not mocked; for whatever a man sows, this he will also reap. [8] For the one who sows to his own flesh will from the flesh reap corruption, but the one who sows to the Spirit will from the Spirit reap eternal life.

Colossians 3:5-8 ~ [5] Therefore consider the members of your earthly body as dead to immorality, impurity, passion, evil desire, and greed, which amounts to idolatry. [6] For it is because of these things that the wrath of God will come upon the sons of disobedience, [7] and in them you also once walked, when you were living in them. [8] But now you also, put them all aside: anger, wrath, malice, slander, *and* abusive speech from your mouth.

At this time, please consider what you've read and learned, and journal your own personal response to this. This can be of great help in the future to see how you are progressing and changing.

3. Who can help me see my errors?

Psalm 139:1-2 ~ [1] O LORD, You have searched me and known *me*. [2] You know when I sit down and when I rise up; You understand my thought from afar.

"How consoling to a child in the dark is the hand of a father or mother, and God's is a Father's hand, not a policeman's." ~ W. Scroggie

Psalm 139:23-24 ~ [23] Search me, O God, and know my heart; Try me and know my anxious thoughts; [24] And see if there be any hurtful way in me, and lead me in the everlasting way.

"It is as when a housewife cleans her chamber. She looks, and there is no dust; the air is clear, and all her furniture is shining brightly. But there is a chink in the window shutter, a ray of light creeps in, and you see the dust dancing up and down, thousands of grains, in the sunbeam. It is all over the room the same, but she can see it only where the sunbeam comes. It is just so with us. God sends a ray of divine light into the heart, and then we see how full of iniquity it is." ~ C. H. Spurgeon

Proverbs 21:2 ~ [2] Every man's way is right in his own eyes, but the LORD weighs the hearts.

If we were our own judge, nobody would be condemned! Which is why we have each been called to be a witness. We have not been called to be the judge, the jury, or the lawyer. HE doesn't need us to argue HIS case or make a plea for HIM. HE is The Judge and HE is the Jury as well as the executioner should we choose death over Life more abundantly.

Hebrews 4:13 ~ [13] And there is no creature hidden from His sight, but all things are open and laid bare to the eyes of Him with whom we have to do.

"The omniscience of God follows from his omnipresence. As God fills Heaven and earth, all things are transacted in his presence. He knows our thoughts far better than they are known to ourselves. We pray to a God Who knows our state and wants, Who hears what we say, and Who is able to meet all our necessities." ~ C. Hodge

At this time, please consider what you've read and learned, and journal your own personal response to this. This can be of great help in the future to see how you are progressing and changing.

4. What means will GOD use to help me see myself?

Psalm 119:130 ~ [130] The unfolding of Your words gives light; It gives understanding to the simple.

"The Word of God is the outward & ordinary means by which the Spirit of God enlightens the understanding of all that are sanctified. We begin to see when we begin to study the Word of God." ~ M. Henry

Hebrews 4:12 ~ [12] For the word of God is living and active and sharper than any two-edged sword, and piercing as far as the division of soul and spirit, of both joints and marrow, and able to judge the thoughts and intentions of the heart.

The Bible is the mirror that shows us our stains, and JESUS' Blood is The Fountain that washes them away.

James 1:5 ~ [5] But if any of you lacks wisdom, let him ask of God, who gives to all generously and without reproach, and it will be given to him.

"Not only was the Holy Spirit active in the writing of the biblical books, he is also active in conveying the truth of the Bible to the minds of those who read it. So, we must pray as we read the Scriptures, and we must ask the Holy Spirit to do His work of enlightenment in our hearts. The Spirit's presence is not given to us to make a careful and diligent study of the Word of God unnecessary. He is given to make our study effective." ~ J. M. Boice

"We should make earnest supplication to God to give us clear minds and pure hearts to overcome our prejudices. We should also pray that God will assist us to overcome our proclivity for slothfulness and make us diligent students of Scripture." ~ R. C. Sproul

1 John 5:14-15 ~ [14] This is the confidence which we have before Him, that, if we ask anything according to His will, He hears us. [15] And if we know that He hears us *in* whatever we ask, we know that we have the requests which we have asked from Him.

Lamentations 3:40-41 ~ [40] Let us examine and probe our ways, and let us return to the LORD. [41] We lift up our heart and hands toward God in heaven

Haggai 1:7 ~ [7] Thus says the LORD of hosts, "Consider your ways!"

Making your extremely transparent and very humbling moral inventory and doing so "fearlessly" does not mean that this process will be painless.

Fearless means that we may be frightened but we go ahead and take our inventory, nevertheless. Fearlessness is openness and honesty in looking within.

2Corinthians 13:5 ~ [5] Test yourselves *to see* if you are in the faith; examine yourselves! Or do you not recognize this about yourselves, that Jesus Christ is in you—unless indeed you fail the test?

"He who has gazed at his own sinfulness will be able to persevere in the face of setbacks. He will not be surprised by the sins of those to whom he ministers; he will weep for the sins of his companions as well as his own sins; but he will not despair because of them, for he has a realistic view of himself. What is more, he has a glorious view of God, and of His power to save and keep." ~ S. B. Ferguson

Galatians 6:3-4 ~ [3] For if anyone thinks he is something when he is nothing, he deceives himself. [4] But each one must examine his own work, and then he will have *reason for* boasting in regard to himself alone, and not in regard to another.

At this time, please consider what you've read and learned, and journal your own personal response to this. This can be of great help in the future to see how you are progressing and changing.

5. What should I consider as I make my moral inventory?

Matthew 22:37-39 ~ ³⁷ And He said to him, "'YOU SHALL LOVE THE LORD YOUR GOD WITH ALL YOUR HEART, AND WITH ALL YOUR SOUL, AND WITH ALL YOUR MIND.' ³⁸ This is the great and foremost commandment. ³⁹ The second is like it, 'YOU SHALL LOVE YOUR NEIGHBOR AS YOURSELF.'

We are not given the option of loving GOD "*or*" our neighbor. We are commanded to Love GOD Almighty "*and*" our neighbor as ourselves.

By the way, we are also not given the opportunity to Love our enemy. We are commanded to! Just saying.

Consider these things, and then it will be much easier to dive deep into yourself and write down those things you have tried so long to keep hidden and secret.

"Do we love God with all our heart, and soul, and strength, and mind? Do we love our neighbor as ourselves? Where is the person who could say with perfect truth, 'I do?'. The best of us, however holy we may be, come far short of perfection. Passages like this should teach us our need of Christ's blood and righteousness. To Him we must go, if we would ever stand with boldness at the bar of God. From Him we must seek grace, that the love of God and man may become the ruling principles of our lives." ~ J. C. Ryle

John 8:31 ~ ³¹ So Jesus was saying to those Jews who had believed Him, "If you continue in My word, *then* you are truly disciples of Mine

"We do not love Jesus at all if He is not our King of kings and Lord of lords. Love Him, and belittle Him! Follow your own will in preference to His will, and then talk of love to Him! Ridiculous." ~ C. H. Spurgeon

1 John 4:20-21 ~ [20] If someone says, "I love God," and hates his brother, he is a liar; for the one who does not love his brother whom he has seen, cannot love God whom he has not seen. [21] And this commandment we have from Him, that the one who loves God should love his brother also.

1 John 5:2-3 ~ [2] By this we know that we love the children of God, when we love God and observe His commandments. [3] For this is the love of God, that we keep His commandments; and His commandments are not burdensome.

At this time, please consider what you've read and learned, and journal your own personal response to this. This can be of great help in the future to see how you are progressing and changing.

6. What is Love?

Romans 13:8 ~ [8] Owe nothing to anyone except to love one another; for he who loves his neighbor has fulfilled *the* law.

Romans 13:10 ~ [10] Love does no wrong to a neighbor; therefore love is the fulfillment of *the* law.

John 14:15 ~ [15] If you love Me, you will keep My commandments

Love is Obedience. Love HIM? Obey HIM!

We dare not direct our lives by our thoughts and feelings. They have been distorted by our sinful nature. We must trust our FATHER'S Instruction in The Holy Bible, HIS Infallible and Inerrant Word. We must follow the example laid out before us, in JESUS The CHRIST.

1Corinthians 13:4-7 ~ [4] Love is patient, love is kind *and* is not jealous; love does not brag *and* is not arrogant, [5] does not act unbecomingly; it does not seek its own, is not provoked, does not take into account a wrong *suffered*, [6] does not rejoice in unrighteousness, but rejoices with the truth; [7] bears all things, believes all things, hopes all things, endures all things.

At this time, please consider what you've read and learned, and journal your own personal response to this. This can be of great help in the future to see how you are progressing and changing.

7. What should I consider beside my deeds when I make my moral inventory?

Psalm 12:3-4 ~ ³ May the LORD cut off all flattering lips, the tongue that speaks great things; ⁴ Who have said, "With our tongue we will prevail; Our lips are our own; who is lord over us?"

"We are moral beings and as such we must accept the consequences of every deed done and every word spoken." ~ A. W. Tozer

Isaiah 6:5 ~ ⁵ Then I said, "Woe is me, for I am ruined! Because I am a man of unclean lips, and I live among a people of unclean lips; For my eyes have seen the King, the LORD of hosts."

"When I was a boy, the old country doctor came lumbering in with his bulging pill-bag and always began his examination by saying, 'Let me see your tongue.' It is a good way to begin the examination of any Christian. What we talk about is a good index to our character. Our speech betrays us." ~ V. Havner

Matthew 12:34-36 ~ ³⁴ You brood of vipers, how can you, being evil, speak what is good? For the mouth speaks out of that which fills the heart. ³⁵ The good man brings out of *his* good treasure what is good; and the evil man brings out of *his* evil treasure what is evil. ³⁶ But I tell you that every careless word that people speak, they shall give an accounting for it in the day of judgment.

Ephesians 5:3-4 ~ ³ But immorality or any impurity or greed must not even be named among you, as is proper among saints; ⁴ and *there must be no* filthiness and silly talk, or coarse jesting, which are not fitting, but rather giving of thanks.

"An evil tongue hath a great influence upon other members. When a man speaketh evil, he will commit it. When the tongue hath the boldness to talk of sin, the rest of the members have the boldness to act it. First we think, than speak, and then do." ~ Thomas Manton

Proverbs 4:23 ~ [23] Watch over your heart with all diligence, for from it *flow* the springs of life.

Dr. M. Laaser says the three building blocks of sexual addiction are fantasy, pornography, and masturbation.

"Fantasy is created by a need to satisfy deep longings. Pornography displays images of how to do that. Masturbation is the physical expression of perhaps the only touching or nurturing the addict receives. The 3 are involved in a cycle."

"Pornography stimulates fantasy. Fantasy needs to be expressed. Masturbation allows a 'release' of that need. There is a problem in this cycle. While it may satisfy the physical need for sex, it never satisfies the emotional and spiritual hunger that rests deep in the soul."

"Addicts have never learned to feed that hunger in a healthy way. Instead, they try to gratify this need in the easiest and most accessible way. Sex allows the addict to escape and thereby cope temporarily with his feelings. More and more sexual activity, however, also creates more and more negative feelings. This vicious cycle makes sexual addiction a very degenerative process. It gets worse." ~ Dr. M. Laaser

"Thoughts are the eggs of words and actions, and within the thoughts lie compacted and condensed all the villainy of actual transgressions." ~ C. H. Spurgeon

Matthew 9:4 ~ [4] And Jesus knowing their thoughts said, "Why are you thinking evil in your hearts?

"Our thoughts are responsible for how we feel and most of what we do. Events occur in our lives, and we usually blame what we feel or how we act on these events. But events, as they are perceived by us, are interpreted in our thoughts. This inner conversation with ourselves is what causes us to feel what we feel and do much of what we do. Our experiences are processed in our thoughts and given meaning before we feel a certain way or respond in a certain way." ~ D. Stoop

Philippians 4:8 ~ [8] Finally, brethren, whatever is true, whatever is honorable, whatever is right, whatever is pure, whatever is lovely, whatever is of good repute, if there is any excellence and if anything worthy of praise, dwell on these things.

Sin is a word, deed, or action (desire) that is in direct deliberate opposition to our Creator. Sin is ever-present every single time a man tries to separate himself from GOD, takes the reins himself believing himself to be powerful and refuses to accept the fact that he is not only powerless but dependent on his Creator.

We must take on a very open, honest and transparent attitude to be able to complete this extremely transparent and humbling moral inventory. Transparency is key. We will find that out in Method 5.

Luke 18:1-2 ~ [1] Now He was telling them a parable to show that at all times they ought to pray and not to lose heart, [2] saying, "In a certain city there was a judge who did not fear God and did not respect man."

"Contempt" is defined as the act of despising, the condition of having no respect, concern, or regard for something or someone. It's the belief that a person is only of importance as he or she satisfies my needs or wishes.

"I could not relate to men, I envied them, but I also despised them. At times, I wished that 'I had what they had.' Sometimes this desire became sexually confused until I thought I wanted them, not what they possessed." ~ E. Hurst

Have many of us have been subconsciously trying to possess the manhood or womanhood we feel we don't have by acting out sexually with the very ones we want to be like? Isn't it evil and futile to use another sexually for such a purpose?

Philippians 2:4-11 ~ [4] do not *merely* look out for your own personal interests, but also for the interests of others. [5] Have this attitude in yourselves which was also in Christ Jesus, [6] who, although He existed in the form of God, did not regard equality with God a thing to be grasped, [7] but emptied Himself, taking the form of a bond-servant, *and* being made in the likeness of men.

[8] Being found in appearance as a man, He humbled Himself by becoming obedient to the point of death, even death on a cross. [9] For this reason also, God highly exalted Him, and bestowed on Him the name which is above every name, [10] so that at the name of Jesus EVERY KNEE WILL BOW, of those who are in heaven and on earth and under the earth, [11] and that every tongue will confess that Jesus Christ is Lord, to the glory of God the Father.

Will you treat others as objects to use or as human beings to respect?

1Peter 2:17 ~ [17] Honor all people, love the brotherhood, fear God, honor the king.

At this time, please consider what you've read and learned, and journal your own personal response to this. This can be of great help in the future to see how you are progressing and changing.

The words "moral inventory" and "extremely transparent and very humbling", tossed in there with "fearlessly" can certainly be frightening.

I was hurting and did not want, did not know if I could bear, any more pain. But I knew I had to make my first attempt, so, I dove in.

As I thought on what I had discovered, I saw that the real force behind my thoughts and feelings, as well as my activities, was not love. It was not that I did not care for those with whom I was involved, but fear had fused with and corrupted that emotion until it had become a grasping, clutching distortion of itself. I was in lust with them!

Am I now fear free? I fear I'm not. I do not claim perfection. This walk is a process, from Glory to Glory. This Faith walk ain't no cake walk!

My moral inventory helped me spot a problem, well, many problems. I am still working on them piece by piece. I see progress, and much of that progress I was Blessed to see through keeping a journal while I went along this very path that The LORD has had me to pen for you. I feel more secure. So, I rejoice!

Helpful Hints

1) Set a time with a brother or sister, and a group if possible, to hear your moral inventory even before you begin to make it. This will help you focus on getting the step done and will give you someone, or someones, you can seek help should you run into difficulty. You alone can make your moral inventory, but you don't have to make it alone!

2) Your inventory will not be the same as everyone else's, nor will you write it and complete it the same way. There is no template for this method. We just take our journal, or a separate notebook (I used a separate notebook, a 3-subject one and I filled it totally), and begin writing things down. Whether words, thoughts, acts, scenarios, whatever.... this will be different for everyone.

3) As you make your inventory, remember these words:

Arise, my soul, arise,
Shake off thy guilty fears:
The bleeding Sacrifice
In my behalf appears:
Before the Throne my Surety stands,
My name is written on His hands!

Five bleeding wounds He bears,
Received on Calvary;
They pour effectual prayers,
They strongly plead for me;
Forgive him, O forgive, they cry,
Nor let that ransomed sinner die! ~ by C. Wesley ~

Method 5. ~ Admit to others, those deepest darkest secrets that were confessed to GOD, and relate to our moral inventory.

Purpose 5. ~ We utilize the inventory from Method 4 to help us when we admit (confess) to others, those deepest darkest secrets that we confessed to GOD Alone in Method 1.

For some of us; habits, strongholds, vices and sin mean shame, hiding, masks, and deception. Some of us, especially those indulging in some dark and secretive activity, even take pride in our ability to keep things "under wraps" and to keep our feelings hidden.

This only allows us to continue in denial. And it is that type of thinking, that type of attitude, that type of ignorance, which helps to convince us that we would never have to deal with the consequences of our actions. It even lets us talk ourselves into believing that there is either nothing wrong with what we're doing or that there is no such thing as consequences.

Luke 8:17 says, "For nothing is hidden that will not become evident, nor anything secret that will not be known and come to light." The Truth can only be kept at bay for so long. The time will come when we can no longer hide the destructiveness of our sinful ways, not even from ourselves.

Most of us were being hurt and we were hurting others, often in the name of love or lust. Hiding merely increases our sense of isolation while also destroying our self-esteem and our feeling of any worth at all. Eventually, we must realize that the secrets we are keeping are keeping us from the Freedom that is available to us.

What we need, if we are ever going to recover, is JESUS The CHRIST. And once we have accepted, embraced, and surrendered to JESUS, then we are recovered, not "in recovery". The biggest lie of addiction is that once an addict, always an addict. That is a lie from the pit of hell designed to keep a hold of you while also providing you with an excuse to "act out" or "stumble". Much the same as calling addiction a "disease", another lie from the pit of hell!!

Then, after we have embraced YESHUA, JESUS The CHRIST, we must discover our true identity in HIM. And in order to discover who we were intended and Created to be in HIM, what we need is to uncover the true meaning of unconditional love.

It was our dishonesty and faithlessness that made receiving such love impossible. To know that kind of love, we must reveal ourselves—ugly warts and all--to GOD, and to ourselves, and then to others. Confession (transparency) is the key that turns the lock on that door which has kept us isolated and vulnerable. It may also be the key that unlocks someone else's door of secrets and shame.

Our moral inventory (Method 4) told us even more about our own selves than we ever thought possible. We began with confessing to GOD Almighty because HE is Love (1John 4:16) and has bound HIMSELF to forgive and cleanse all who confess to HIM (1John 1:9). We can be certain of HIS response!

Our acceptance of HIS Forgiveness empowers us to face ourselves in a new way. Knowing HIS Forgiveness enables us to move past our pain.

Knowing The FATHER'S Acceptance enables us to accept ourselves, which includes our intended identity found only in JESUS The CHRIST.

This prepares us for a full, bold, sometimes scary but very honest confession to others. This is vital, and very difficult, if we are to ever break those patterns of dishonesty and isolation.

Unless we take this step, we can never break through the terrible isolation that keeps us from what we have craved all along, that intimacy, the unconditional love and acceptance which can only come from The One Who knows all that we are and have done.

RESIDUE is defined as; "That which remains after a part is taken, separated, or removed."

When something remains, it is due to our own actions, or inactions. I tell young men that are in "recovery" homes & groups that unless they confess, and speak, their deepest darkest secrets and confess what they did to get the drugs, or what they did while they were on the drugs, they would never be totally Free.

It is RESIDUE! And eventually that RESIDUE will permeate their skin and draw them back to that sinful place, and usually deeper, darker, and deadlier than before.

It is so very important to share our deepest and darkest secrets. For men, with their brothers and for women, their sisters, and eventually, if/when possible, in a testimony or co-ed group setting. It is usually not a good idea in the beginning for men to share with women or vice versa.

This method comes so late in the RESIDUE guide because of the strength and passion for Freedom this step takes.

The first person we choose to confess to, because many will not be able to do so in front of a group until they can do so comfortably with one or two others, should have some understanding of us. This person must understand our sins, our habits, our strongholds, and addictions.

This person, or these persons, should be able to keep our disclosures completely confidential (until we are ready to share more openly to others), should have a good sense of his/her own weaknesses and need of Grace, and should have also experienced the unconditional Love of GOD The FATHER through HIS Son, JESUS The CHRIST, our LORD & SAVIOR.

When we confess our deepest and darkest secrets, putting our "personal" and "secretive" lives out there, we must do so with the idea that it is not something we do "in confidence"! This means that the goal is that eventually we cannot keep these secrets from some but only share with others. We need these things to be released, spoken out, and given up so they hold no more power over us.

Confession builds intimacy which is an important part of discovering our intended identity in YESHUA, JESUS The CHRIST, but we must be aware of our own vulnerabilities. Those who have remained in RESIDUE for this long are now invested in themselves, others, and their walk, which is another reason this method comes so late in the program.

Confession is not an "X-rated" recounting of every sordid detail of our sexual misconduct, but it is an honest facing of our character defects which have made us defenseless against the lusts of our flesh. We need to face our internal motivations, the excitement we received from our sexual and moral depravity, rather than to recount titillating details of sexual encounters.

Confession is not a "blame game". While our struggles came to most of us as a result of things which happened in our childhood, we are responsible for our responses to these things as adults. Confession means facing our own faults, not the faults of others.

The person/s to whom we make our confession can help us put what we reveal in proper perspective. If we are being too easy with ourselves, he/she can help us see through our rationalizations so that the Truth can make us free. If we are being too hard on ourselves, feeling that everything that has ever gone wrong is all our fault, we can be helped to see what we are responsible for and leave to others that for which they are accountable.

Many of us have kept our lives rigorously closed for years, and this first experience of sharing ourselves with another in complete honesty can call forth differing responses. Some of us have found it wonderfully liberating; others find it very painful. Some are greatly embarrassed while others sincerely believe that there is nothing "really wrong" with it.

No matter what our reaction at first, all of us have found in time that, in making our confession and being transparent, we turn a major corner in discovering who we are intended and

Created to be. We take a very large step which can enable us never again to live closed, divided, loveless, fearful lives.

Many believe their deepest secrets about what they did to satisfy the lusts of their flesh can never come out or it could ruin their relationship, reputation and even the way others treat them.

Stop this deadly train of thought now! <u>Just Stop It!!</u> This is a part of a very customized tool that GOD Almighty has allowed you to obtain, and you'd better use it! Even after we have ignored HIM, dissed HIM, cussed HIM, ran from HIM, etc.... HE still allowed each one of us to obtain a very powerful tool; a customized weapon; that would allow us to reveal HIS Glory when we became ready.

This tool, or weapon, is your testimony! This tool could help lead many others around you out of their own darkness!

Revelation 12:11 ~ And they overcame him because of the blood of the Lamb and because of the word of their testimony, and they did not love their life even when faced with death.

Right there in The Word of GOD Almighty, your very own testimony is compared side by side with The Blood of The Lamb! Does that tell you how powerful your testimony can be? It should! Because your testimony could be the very GoOD News that someone needs to hear to encourage them to come out of that darkness and call on HIS Precious and Holy Name!

1. What should I do about those wrongs and the heinous things I discovered when I made my moral inventory?

Psalm 32:5 ~ [5] I acknowledged my sin to You, and my iniquity I did not hide; I said, "I will confess my transgressions to the LORD"; And You forgave the guilt of my sin. *Selah.*

James 5:16 ~ Therefore, confess your sins to one another, and pray for one another so that you may be healed. The effective prayer of a righteous man can accomplish much.

"...when I have sinned, I have an immediate reluctance to go to Christ. I am ashamed to go. I feel as if it would do no good to go, as if it were making Christ a minister of sin, to go straight from the swine-trough to the best robe, and a thousand other excuses; but I'm persuaded that they are all lies, direct from hell. I am sure there is neither peace nor safety from deeper sin, but in going directly to the Lord Jesus Christ. This is God's way of peace and holiness. It is folly to the world and the beclouded heart, but it is The Way." ~ R. M. McCheyne

Proverbs 28:13 ~ [13] He who conceals his transgressions will not prosper, but he who confesses and forsakes *them* will find compassion.

"No amount of falls will really undo us if we keep on picking ourselves up each time. We shall of course be very muddy and tattered children by the time we reach home, but the bathrooms are all ready, the towels put out, and the clean clothes in the airing cupboard. The only fatal thing is to lose one's temper and give it up. It is when we notice the dirt that God is present in us: it is the very sign of His presence." ~ C. S. Lewis

Jeremiah 14:20 ~ [20] We know our wickedness, O LORD, the iniquity of our fathers, for we have sinned against You.

Our moral inventory has allowed us to see the characteristics that have stemmed from our lusts, choices, and addictions. Now transparency is the key to open the next door to continue on this path of Freedom in HIM.

1John 1:9 ~ [9] If we confess our sins, He is faithful and righteous to forgive us our sins and to cleanse us from all unrighteousness

The only attitude toward sin that we can have, that we must have, is that we do not deny it or hide it but we speak it aloud to release the power it holds over us so that we can receive the healing that comes with the forgiveness that YAHWEH, our Heavenly FATHER, has promised us.

Jeremiah 31:19 ~ [19] 'For after I turned back, I repented; And after I was instructed, I smote on *my* thigh; I was ashamed and also humiliated because I bore the reproach of my youth.'

"He that never mourned for sin has never rejoiced in the Lord. If I can look back on my past life and say, 'I have no grief over it,' then I should do the same again if I had the opportunity. And this shows that my heart is as perverse as ever." ~ C. H. Spurgeon

Ezekiel 36:31 ~ [31] Then you will remember your evil ways and your deeds that were not good, and you will loathe yourselves in your own sight for your iniquities and your abominations.

"Repentance is among other things a sincere apology to God for distrusting Him so long, and faith is throwing oneself upon Christ in complete confidence." ~ A. W. Tozer

Daniel 10:8-12 ~ [8] So I was left alone and saw this great vision; yet no strength was left in me, for my natural color turned to a deathly pallor, and I retained no strength. [9] But I heard the sound of his words; and as soon as I heard the sound of his words, I fell into a deep sleep on my face, with my face to the ground.

[10] Then behold, a hand touched me and set me trembling on my hands and knees. [11] He said to me, "O Daniel, man of high esteem, understand the words that I am about to tell you and stand upright, for I have now been sent to you." And when he had spoken this word to me, I stood up trembling.

[12] Then he said to me, "Do not be afraid, Daniel, for from the first day that you set your heart on understanding *this* and on humbling yourself before your God, your words were heard, and I have come in response to your words.

How many of us thought we were happy with our lives and things were just the way they were and there was nothing we could about them? It is ironic because I can remember thinking I was happy, saying I was happy, even acting happy, but all along I knew there was something not quite right and that I longed for something more. I knew, deep down, that I was not that "happy person" I pretended to be.

I was totally out of touch with myself and didn't even know it. I was out of touch with my own feelings, in a sense, ever since I was a child.

How else can we avoid pain but to deny that we feel it and sometimes even misconstrue that pain for pleasure just to be able to remain "happy."

There were many times I cried and cried, then was angry and wanted to hurt another person so that I could feel better. Make sense? Sound familiar? It did to me at the time. I have verbally and physically attacked and hurt people just to prove to them how "happy" I was.

B. Earl puts it like this, very realistically I might add, he says, "It was like someone inside me was screaming at me to wake up, someone trapped in a cave-in, yelling out, hoping the rescuers will hear. But I had no idea how to listen, who was screaming, what the screams meant, or what to do. I was afraid. There are two very definite reasons why for years I wanted no part of the truth."

"One, I believed I was 'fundamentally bad, inadequate, defective, unworthy, and not fully valid as a human being.' Two, on an intuitive level, I knew truth meant pain. I believed that feeling pain was bad and meant something was wrong with me. Getting down to the core of you--who you really are--is achieved by peeling off one painful layer of oppression at a time. Today I know pain is the doorway to freedom. I'm not necessarily thrilled with that reality, but it's the truth."

At this time, please consider what you've read and learned, and journal your own personal response to this. This can be of great help in the future to see how you are progressing and changing.

2. Do I absolutely need to confess my wrongs to another human being?

Joshua 7:19-20 ~ [19] Then Joshua said to Achan, "My son, I implore you, give glory to the LORD, the God of Israel, and give praise to Him; and tell me now what you have done. Do not hide it from me." [20] So Achan answered Joshua and said, "Truly, I have sinned against the LORD, the God of Israel, and this is what I did

There is an old saying, "you are only as sick as your secrets". I find this to be very true. JESUS said the whole have no need of a doctor, only the sick do.

If you can get through this method without truly and honestly opening up about your deepest darkest most taboo secrets, lusts, strongholds, fantasies, addictions, etc... then you will certainly try to do so. Fact is, you mustn't!

Not if you truly want Freedom. To confess to YAHWEH, GOD Almighty is one thing, but to confess and be transparent to other human beings, that is where the power comes in and the chains start breaking and will rattle no more!

2Samuel 12:13 ~ [13] Then David said to Nathan, "I have sinned against the LORD." And Nathan said to David, "The LORD also has taken away your sin; you shall not die."

Even A/A and N/A participants, clean for years, often pay dearly for not being bold or brave enough to confess one to another.

They have no problem telling of how they carried the load alone; how much they suffered of irritability, anxiety, remorse, and depression; and how, unconsciously seeking relief, they would sometimes accuse even their best friends of the very character defects they themselves were trying to conceal.

They always discover that freedom, or relief, never come by confessing the sins of other people, because everybody has to confess his/her own.

This method is detrimental. Confessing our deepest and darkest secrets challenges our beliefs that if someone really knew everything about us that we would probably be rejected. With the unconditional acceptance of another human being there is an amazing release of pain that comes from such confession.

Acts 19:18 ~ [18] Many also of those who had believed kept coming, confessing, and disclosing their practices.

We think that we would be weak and vulnerable if we confess. Scripture says that YAHWEH is strong when we are weak. It is okay to be weak and vulnerable, as long as you understand it is part of the process to becoming strong and mighty in The LORD GOD Almighty!

James 5:16 ~ [16] Therefore, confess your sins to one another, and pray for one another so that you may be healed. The effective prayer of a righteous man can accomplish much.

"A man who confesses his sins in the presence of a brother knows that he is no longer alone with himself; he experiences the presence of God in the reality of the other person. As long as I am by myself in the confession of my sins, everything remains in the dark, but in the presence of a brother, the sin has to be brought into the light." ~ D. Bonhoeffer

At this time, please consider what you've read and learned, and journal your own personal response to this. This can be of great help in the future to see how you are progressing and changing.

3. Can't I just correct my defects of character on my own?

Job 14:4 ~ [4] Who can make the clean out of the unclean? No one!

"God helps those who cannot help themselves." ~ C. H. Spurgeon

Proverbs 20:9 ~ [9] Who can say, "I have cleansed my heart, I am pure from my sin"?

"The way of sin is down-hill; men not only cannot stop themselves, but the longer they continue in it, the faster they run." ~ M. Henry

Men hate their sins but cannot leave them.

Romans 8:7-8 ~ [7] because the mind set on the flesh is hostile toward God; for it does not subject itself to the law of God, for it is not even able *to do so*, [8] and those who are in the flesh cannot please God.

Titus 3:3-7 ~ [3] For we also once were foolish ourselves, disobedient, deceived, enslaved to various lusts and pleasures, spending our life in malice and envy, hateful, hating one another. [4] But when the kindness of God our Savior and *His* love for mankind appeared, [5] He saved us, not on the basis of deeds which we have done in righteousness, but according to His mercy, by the washing of regeneration and renewing by the Holy Spirit, [6] whom He poured out upon us richly through Jesus Christ our Savior, [7] so that being justified by His grace we would be made heirs according to *the* hope of eternal life.

Psalm 25:7-12 ~ [7] Do not remember the sins of my youth or my transgressions; According to Your lovingkindness remember me, for Your goodness' sake, O LORD. [8] Good and upright is the LORD; Therefore He instructs sinners in the way.

[9] He leads the humble in justice, and He teaches the humble His way. [10] All the paths of the LORD are lovingkindness and truth to those who keep His covenant and His testimonies.

[11] For Your name's sake, O LORD, pardon my iniquity, for it is great. [12] Who is the man who fears the LORD? He will instruct him in the way he should choose.

"Though you have struggled in vain against your evil habits, though you have wrestled with them sternly, and resolved, and re-resolved, only to be defeated by your giant sins and your terrible passions, there is One who can conquer all your sins for you. He can make and keep you pure within. O, look to Him!" ~ C. H. Spurgeon

Psalm 51:10 ~ [10] Create in me a clean heart, O God, and renew a steadfast spirit within me.

"A holy man is the workmanship of the Holy Spirit." ~ C. H. Spurgeon

Ezekiel 11:19-20 ~ [19] And I will give them one heart, and put a new spirit within them. And I will take the heart of stone out of their flesh and give them a heart of flesh, [20] that they may walk in My statutes and keep My ordinances and do them. Then they will be My people, and I shall be their God.

"The first link between my soul and Christ is, not my goodness, but my badness; not my merit, but my misery; not my standing, but my falling; not my riches, but my need. He comes to visit His people, yet not to admire their beauties, but to remove their deformities; not to reward their virtues, but to forgive their sins. Go to Him as sinners and cry, 'O Lord Jesus, I need thy salvation.' Only believe in Him, and He will be your salvation." C. H. Spurgeon

This quote from Spurgeon makes me think of John 3:16 ~ [16] For God so loved the world, that He gave His only begotten Son, that whoever believes in Him shall not perish, but have eternal life.

Many have tried to warp this passage severely taking away from what the passage says in actuality and reality, and most importantly, in Truth.

Some attempt to take the word "kosmos" (world) here to refer to "the elect." But that is absolute nonsense, as is the false and dangerous doctrine of "the elect."

All of the evidence of the usage of the word "kosmos", or "world", in John's Gospel is against the suggestion of it referring to "the elect." The word does not so much refer to "bigness" as it does to "badness."

In John's vocabulary, world is primarily the moral order in willful and culpable rebellion against GOD. So GOD'S Love in coming to this earth, robing HIMSELF in flesh, to become the man JESUS The CHRIST is to be admired not because it is extended to so big a thing as the world, but to so bad a thing; not to so many people, but more to such wicked people.

Matthew 1:21 ~ 21 She will bear a Son; and you shall call His name Jesus, for He will save His people from their sins.

John 3:5-7 ~ 5 Jesus answered, "Truly, truly, I say to you, unless one is born of water and the Spirit he cannot enter into the kingdom of God. 6 That which is born of the flesh is flesh, and that which is born of the Spirit is spirit. 7 Do not be amazed that I said to you, 'You must be born again.'

"Men do not become Christian by association with church people, nor by religious contact, nor by religious education; they become Christian only by an invasion of their nature by the Spirit of God in the New Birth." ~ A. W. Tozer

"The new birth makes us partakers of the divine nature. There the work of undoing the dissimilarity between us and God begins. The New birth does not produce the finished product. The new being that is born of God is as far from completeness as the new baby born an hour ago." ~ A. W. Tozer

Galatians 5:16 ~ 16 But I say, walk by the Spirit, and you will not carry out the desire of the flesh.

2Thessalonians 3:3 ~ 3 But the Lord is faithful, and He will strengthen and protect you from the evil *one*.

At this time, please take it all in and journal your own personal response to what you are thinking & feeling. This can be of great help in the future to see how you are progressing and changing.

4. What must I do to get free from my defects of character?

Psalm 91:14-15 ~ [14] "Because he has loved Me, therefore I will deliver him; I will set him *securely* on high, because he has known My name. [15] "He will call upon Me, and I will answer him; I will be with him in trouble; I will rescue him and honor him.

"Prayer is the key of heaven, and faith is the hand that turns it." ~ T. Watson

Psalm 145:18-19 ~ [18] The LORD is near to all who call upon Him, to all who call upon Him in truth. [19] He will fulfill the desire of those who fear Him; He will also hear their cry and will save them

We must kneel before we can stand upright.

Jeremiah 33:3 ~ [3] 'Call to Me and I will answer you, and I will tell you great and mighty things, which you do not know.'

Matthew 7:7-11 ~ [7] "Ask, and it will be given to you; seek, and you will find; knock, and it will be opened to you. [8] For everyone who asks receives, and he who seeks finds, and to him who knocks it will be opened. [9] Or what man is there among you who, when his son asks for a loaf, will give him a stone? [10] Or if he asks for a fish, he will not give him a snake, will he? [11] If you then, being evil, know how to give good gifts to your children, how much more will your Father who is in heaven give what is good to those who ask Him!

"I ought to pray before seeing anyone. Often when I sleep long, or meet with others early, and then have family prayer, and breakfast, and forenoon callers, often it is eleven or twelve o'clock before I begin secret prayer. This is a wretched system. It is unscriptural. Christ rose before day, and went into a solitary place. David says, 'Early will I seek Thee; Thou shalt early hear my voice.' Family prayer loses much of its power and sweetness; and I can do no good to those who come to seek from me. The conscience feels guilty, the soul unfed, the lamp not trimmed. Then, when secret prayer comes, the soul is often out of tune. I feel it is far better to begin with God--to seek His face first--to get my soul near Him before it is near another." ~ R. M. McCheyne

John 16:24 ~ Hitherto have ye asked nothing in my name: ask, and ye shall receive, that your joy may be full.

Jeremiah 29:11-13 ~ [11] For I know the plans that I have for you,' declares the LORD, 'plans for welfare and not for calamity to give you a future and a hope. [12] Then you will call upon Me and come and pray to Me, and I will listen to you. [13] You will seek Me and find *Me* when you search for Me with all your heart.

John 15:7 ~ [7] If you abide in Me, and My words abide in you, ask whatever you wish, and it will be done for you.

"If you would have God hear you when you pray, you must hear Him when He speaks." ~ T. Brooks

Hebrews 10:36 ~ [36] For you have need of endurance, so that when you have done the will of God, you may receive what was promised.

Many find it impossible that they can admit the very things they tried so hard to keep secret and feel better. They kept it hidden because they believed it would cause much grief and chaos in their lives.

How many men do you know that can stand in front of a group of men and women and tell them how he became a molester of boys? How many men do you know that would dare admit to being a pedophile? How many men could you imagine speaking with a microphone, over a large PA system telling of how he was not only molested, but how he also "recruited" boys into that darkness?

Not many I am sure.

Well, now you know at least one... me!

At this time, please take it all in and journal your own personal response to what you are thinking & feeling. This can be of great help in the future to see how you are progressing and changing.

Confess my defects of character, especially my deepest, darkest secrets and activities, to another human being?

These were things I'd spent my entire life hiding. They proved beyond a shadow of a doubt that I was defective and that I was depraved and perverted. To reveal these things was to guarantee being held in contempt, despised, sneered at, rejected, spat upon!

I did a 6-week experiment in a men's group. I started for the first 5 weeks with the very basics of my sinful life, without sharing the heavy stuff. Each week those men would share the "basics" as well; baby mama drama, drugs, alcohol, anger issues.

The sixth week I told of my being molested and then becoming a molester. Of homosexual and transgender prostitution. Of being HIV+ at age 14. Of my sex addiction, engaging in sexual activity with homeless people in parking lots or alleys. I also told of my lust for young men, especially teenage boys. I told them of how I intentionally and purposely tried to infect as many of those men and boys as I could with HIV.

Once I was finished, each of those men confessed something they'd never ever shared to anyone before, not even to GOD. They spoke their deep dark heavy secrets, and in doing so, they released the power those things held over them. This was the first time I saw a group of men crying, hugging, and sharing of themselves. Powerful! Intimacy!

Working this method was crucial to my discovering my true identity in JESUS The CHRIST. Without it, my working of the steps which went before would have remained ever incomplete. Without it, I wouldn't have been unable to go on.

This method was the most difficult. It was terrifying! But without it, I would never have known unconditional love, true and pure intimacy, which has played a tremendous part in securing the ever-increasing Freedom I am enjoying today.

Helpful Hints

1) Keeping several of GOD'S promises to forgive and cleanse in front of you helps when you first confess your inventory to another. Should uncomfortable feelings remain concerning any item on your moral inventory, be sure to discuss them.

2) Set aside a time to consider your inventory yourself before and after confession. What character defects did you discover? Write your feelings about them in your journal. Know that The FATHER forgives you and accept your identity, as HE accepts you in JESUS The CHRIST, and make a list of the character defects you intend to ask HIM to remove from your life.

3) Confession need not be made all at once but can be done in intervals. Take as much time as you need and stop if you really need to. Set another time and continue until you have shared everything. Remember, you must be completely honest. Hold nothing back. Ask for feedback. Journal your feelings during the process and discuss them.

4) Memorize one of the verses you found helpful in this chapter.

Method 6. Make an amends, when possible/appropriate, to the people we have harmed, hurt, used, and abused.

Purpose 6. Forgiveness. This is not just for us; it is for all involved.

In the past when I wronged someone, I would just not give a darn and look down on them like they were the reason of their misery for allowing me to wrong them or hurt them. However, many wish that it had never happened. Like I just said, some of us didn't even care that we had hurt someone or damaged a relationship. While some did and do.

Now, however, I choose to live in reality by gratefully acknowledging that though I cannot change the past, I can do something about the present.

All we have is right here and right now. The future is not promised. The past is gone. The FATHER has granted the right here and the right now. As my mama used to say, "Yesterday is history, tomorrow a mystery but today is a gift, that is why it is called the present."

In the past, many of us bottled up the guilt we felt when we hurt another person. We often withdrew from that person and sometimes developed deep resentments toward those we had injured. Far from improving matters, withdrawal and resentment only fed the deep fears of abandonment and rejection which had fueled our struggle.

Now it is time for us to learn how to work through our resentments and resolve the problems within our relationships by going directly to the people we have harmed, admitting our wrongs, asking forgiveness, and trying to repair any damage that we have done, if it is at all possible, profitable or advisable.

Obviously, this is not easy! It takes enormous courage to reach out to someone and admit that we have wronged them. Some of us, to spare ourselves the pain of face-to-face contact, will try to find an "easier, softer way". We will seek to make it easier on ourselves, for instance, by writing a letter instead of going directly to the one we have grieved.

This will only document what we are trying to erase and often leave our relationships weighted down with even more misunderstandings than before. Sometimes some people read some messages/letters/texts/etc with an attitude of how they feel either at that moment or about the situation.

Some of us will find that writing a letter is a good way to collect our thoughts. A good idea when using this method, is to personally hand that letter to the one we have wronged, ask them to read it in our presence because we simply cannot find the words we need to express our grief. Then, we try to answer their questions and elaborate on what we wrote.

Some of us have to telephone the one we had wronged because we fear that a face to face meeting might lead to an argument or even a fall. But all of us must realize that there is no substitute for direct contact with the one we have harmed in this difficult but liberating process.

The process itself is a simple one.

First, we make a list of all the people we have harmed and those whom we have manifested resentment, prejudice, or intolerance toward.

Second, we prioritize that list giving first place to those who have been most seriously and most recently hurt.

Third, we explore in writing how we have wronged them and share our findings, asking input on what we have written and guidance as to the wisdom and possibility of making amends.

Fourth, we call the person we hurt and make an appointment to see them.

Fifth, we express our grief at the ways in which we wronged them and our willingness to do whatever we can to make amends. We ask how they feel about what we have shared and what they feel would be an appropriate amends. We earnestly try to follow through on any commitments we make to them.

There are some cautions. Remember, the primary goal is not to relieve our guilt-feelings, but to correct our wrongs. We should never try to make amends when to do so would injure (physical, mental, emotional, or spiritual) another person or ourself.

While our efforts may cause some discomfort, our goal is not our personal ease, but to relieve the suffering of those we have injured or hurt. To make our wrongs right!

We must walk a fine line between rationalizations that keep us from making amends where we can, and folly that leads us to dump our problems on others without weighing the impact on them.

Seek counsel through Prayer, and also from your brethren, as to whether or not it is wise to try to make amends in the first place.

It is also important to remember that making amends is more than simply offering an apology. It includes a commitment to change those attitudes and behaviors which caused the wounds in the first place.

Be sure to include yourself on the list of those you have injured, just as reference. All of us have been our own worst enemies! We make amends to ourselves by not being harsh with ourselves, as we have in the past, and by resolving to walk in The Way and avoid stumbling or falling!

We cannot "forgive ourselves"! That is a huge dangerous misunderstanding as well as a very wrong mindset to put yourself in. King David said that when he sinned, he sinned against YAHWEH, GOD Almighty. When we sin, we sin against GOD Almighty. Only HE can forgive our sin.

If I hurt you, then you can forgive me. But I also must know that I have not only sinned against you, but GOD as well. You must guard against letting this process undermine your newly discovered sense of The FATHER'S acceptance and your own worth before HIM.

1John 1:7 ~ "⁷ but if we walk in the Light as He Himself is in the Light, we have fellowship with one another, and the blood of Jesus His Son cleanses us from all sin."

If you are trusting in JESUS The CHRIST and have laid it all at HIS feet, you are no longer guilty, you are forgiven; you are no longer dirty, you are clean!

Don't punish yourself. To try and punish yourself is to deny the adequacy of HIS sacrifice for you. To try and punish yourself is to tell HIM that HIS forgiveness is not good enough for you.

While we often have to endure some consequences because of our actions, we ought not to add to the misery they have already caused and thus rob GOD Almighty of HIS Glory through this process.

In most instances you will be able to make amends and avoid making the same mistakes again. The goal of this step is healing others' wounds, not inflicting fresh ones on yourself!

Obviously, you may never be able to fix everything you have done wrong, but you can repair some of the damage. Confessing that you hurt someone does not take away their pain, but confessing, accepting responsibility, explaining your struggle, and allowing the person to express his or her feelings opens a line of communication which can lead to an improved relationship.

Remember your limitations. You can only confess the harm you have caused in the past and do your best to behave differently in the future. You cannot control the way others respond to your past actions or your present attempts at making amends.

Realistically, you will not be able to rebuild all of your relationships. Some of those who have been hurt will not want to risk relating to you again.

Forgiveness does not necessarily mean reconciliation. You do all that you can. Their fears are their problem. Others will need lots of time and support before they can forgive or trust you again.

Remember, the purpose of making amends is not to get something, but to ease the pain of those you wounded. And remember, forgiveness does not mean that the relationship has to be mended and go back to the way it was. Sometimes that relationship is best left alone. Forgiveness does not always mean reconciliation.

A few people may make unreasonable demands. They may still be angry and wish to use amends as a way to punish you. If you suspect this, tell the person making the demands that you are sorry for your wrong, but you cannot do all that they ask. Do so and move on!

This whole process teaches us how to deal with new failures as soon as they occur.

1. Does the Bible encourage making amends?

Numbers 5:5-8 ~ 5 Then the LORD spoke to Moses, saying, 6 "Speak to the sons of Israel, 'When a man or woman commits any of the sins of mankind, acting unfaithfully against the LORD, and that person is guilty, 7 then he shall confess his sins which he has committed, and he shall make restitution in full for his wrong and add to it one-fifth of it, and give it to him whom he has wronged. 8 But if the man has no relative to whom restitution may be made for the wrong, the restitution which is made for the wrong must go to the LORD for the priest, besides the ram of atonement, by which atonement is made for him.

The command to bring a ram of atonement teaches us that making amends (our work) is not the same as making the atonement (JESUS' work). We do not make amends in hopes that this will blot out our sins or earn us acceptance with GOD.

We are not our own saviors. YESHUA, JESUS The CHRIST saves! And HIM alone! HE washes us from our sins in HIS Own Blood (Revelation 1:5). Having been forgiven & accepted in JESUS The CHRIST, we make amends to repair as much of the damage that we have done to others as we possibly can.

Proverbs 3:27 ~ 27 Do not withhold good from those to whom it is due, when it is in your power to do it.

Matthew 5:9 ~ 9 Blessed are the peacemakers, for they shall be called sons of God.

Many times, we may have even used sex as a means of escape from our own guilt and emotional pain, even the guilt of hurting & using others.

Making amends gives us the opportunity to gain some standing again. We must learn that when we make a mistake, that we do not have to retreat into those fleshly desires and make-believe fantasy lands of despair.

In most cases, people will accept your efforts to right the wrongs that you have done, and they will also find a new respect for you, although it may take time.

"Peacemakers are not only passively peaceful, like the meek, who keep the peace; but actively peaceful by endeavoring to end contentions, and so make peace." ~ C. H. Spurgeon

Obedience is more important than even worship!

Matthew 5:23-26 ~ [23] Therefore if you are presenting your offering at the altar, and there remember that your brother has something against you, [24] leave your offering there before the altar and go; first be reconciled to your brother, and then come and present your offering. [25] Make friends quickly with your opponent at law while you are with him on the way, so that your opponent may not hand you over to the judge, and the judge to the officer, and you be thrown into prison. [26] Truly I say to you, you will not come out of there until you have paid up the last cent.

I once read this amazing passage by E.H. Plumtre, "Our Lord paints a scene in the Jewish Temple. The worshipper is about to offer a 'gift' and stands at the altar with the priest waiting to do his work. That is the right time for recollection and self-scrutiny.

The worshipper is to ask himself, not whether he has a ground of complaint against anyone, but whether anyone has cause of complaint against him. Has he injured his neighbor by act, or spoken bitter words against him?

To leave the gift and the priest, the act of sacrifice unfinished, would be strange and startling, yet that, our Lord teaches, were better than to sacrifice with the sense of a wrong unconfessed.

There must be confession of wrong and the endeavor to make amends, to bring about, as far as in us lies, reconciliation. The imagery is changed to that of human tribunals.

The man we have wronged appears as the 'adversary,' the prosecutor bringing his charge against us. The impulse of the natural man at such a time, even if conscious of wrong, is to make the best of his case, to prevaricate, to recriminate.

The truer wisdom, Christ teaches, is to 'agree'--better, to be on good terms with--show our own good will and so win his."

Matthew 7:12 ~ [12] In everything, therefore, treat people the same way you want them to treat you, for this is the Law and the Prophets.

"In the Golden Rule the Sermon reaches its climax; it is 'the capstone of the whole discourse.' It is of course assumed that men wish to have done to them what is really good for them: wishes for what is pleasant but harmful are not included. What we desire from our neighbors is love; true, constant, discerning love: and it is from our experience of our own needs in this respect that we can discern how much love of the same kind we owe to others." ~ A. Plummer

Romans 12:18 ~ [18] If possible, so far as it depends on you, be at peace with all men.

We cannot control the responses of others (hence the words "if it is possible"), but we can give our best efforts to make amends (hence the words "as much as depends on you"). That is all YAHWEH, GOD Almighty, expects of each one of us.

Luke 15:11-24 ~ [11] And He said, "A man had two sons. [12] The younger of them said to his father, 'Father, give me the share of the estate that falls to me.' So he divided his wealth between them. [13] And not many days later, the younger son gathered everything together and went on a journey into a distant country, and there he squandered his estate with loose living.

[14] Now when he had spent everything, a severe famine occurred in that country, and he began to be impoverished. [15] So he went and hired himself out to one of the citizens of that country, and he sent him into his fields to feed swine. [16] And he would have gladly filled his stomach with the pods that the swine were eating, and no one was giving anything to him. [17] But when he came to his senses, he said, 'How many of my father's hired men have more than enough bread, but I am dying here with hunger! [18] I will get up and go to my father, and will say to him, "Father, I have sinned against heaven, and in your sight;

19 I am no longer worthy to be called your son; make me as one of your hired men.'" 20 So he got up and came to his father. But while he was still a long way off, his father saw him and felt compassion for him, and ran and embraced him and kissed him. 21 And the son said to him, 'Father, I have sinned against heaven and in your sight; I am no longer worthy to be called your son.'

22 But the father said to his slaves, 'Quickly bring out the best robe and put it on him, and put a ring on his hand and sandals on his feet; 23 and bring the fattened calf, kill it, and let us eat and celebrate; 24 for this son of mine was dead and has come to life again; he was lost and has been found.' And they began to celebrate.

This is the best biblical example of the need for, process of, and desired result in making amends. The prodigal son had wounded his father terribly. The young man's ignorance also caused him deep pain. Pain brought him to his senses. He longed to restore his relationship with his father, so he carefully thought out what he wanted to say and, when they met, used those very words. He did not try to excuse his behavior or minimize his offence. He did not make any claims on his father. He spoke honest, direct, and with a contrite heart.

He acknowledged his guilt and offered to do whatever he could to repair the damage he had done. His father's response was all the son could have asked, and far more than he expected. May you experience all the joy of the forgiveness and reconciliation revealed here!

Acts 19:18-19 ~ [18] Many also of those who had believed kept coming, confessing, and disclosing their practices. [19] And many of those who practiced magic brought their books together and began burning them in the sight of everyone; and they counted up the price of them and found it fifty thousand pieces of silver.

Those who struggle with pornography can learn much from the example of the people of Ephesus. Imagine a bunch of porn addicts and sex addicts bringing books, magazines, computers, laptops, smart phones, etc.... and tossing them all in a huge pile and burning them.

At this time, please consider what you've read and learned, and journal your own personal response to this. This can be of great help in the future to see how you are progressing and changing.

2. Do I need to be afraid of how others might respond?

Psalm 118:6 ~ [6] The LORD is for me; I will not fear; What can man do to me?

Proverbs 16:7 ~ [7] When a man's ways are pleasing to the LORD, He makes even his enemies to be at peace with him.

Only The FATHER in Heaven can turn your foes into your friends.

"God will take care of His people. Peace or war shall turn to their everlasting good." ~ C. Bridges

Romans 8:31 ~ [31] What then shall we say to these things? If God is for us, who is against us"

If Jesus is our righteousness, then no human is better or worse than me. If we fight not against flesh and blood, but against spiritual forces and principalities, then no human is my enemy. If God is my provision, then I don't need to lay up treasures on earth or defensively hoard and protect my possessions.

If God is our creator, then every human is worth knowing, and respecting, and serving as a beautiful, unique, amazing example of God's love and creativity, no matter how poor or socially different from me. If God is my protector, I do not need to be afraid of any change, or any person, or any circumstance." ~ J. Hornsby

2Timothy 1:7 ~ [7] For God has not given us a spirit of fear, but of power and of love and of a sound mind.

"The faint-hearted mistrust themselves and others; and they discourage themselves and others. They anticipate dangers and difficulties, and thereby sometimes create them; and they anticipate failure, and thereby often bring it about." ~ A. Plummer

Hebrews 13:5-6 ~ [5] Make sure that your character is free from the love of money, being content with what you have; for He Himself has said, "I WILL NEVER DESERT YOU, NOR WILL I EVER FORSAKE YOU," [6] so that we confidently say, "THE LORD IS MY HELPER, I WILL NOT BE AFRAID. WHAT WILL MAN DO TO ME?"

At this time, please consider what you've read and learned, and journal your own personal response to this. This can be of great help in the future to see how you are progressing and changing.

3. How am I to respond to those who hurt me?

The beauty of experiencing the response of others to your own wrongs, allow us to see how we should respond to those who have hurt us. We know what we would like for others' response to be, thus showing us what ours should be to them.

Proverbs 15:1 ~ [1] A gentle answer turns away wrath, but a harsh word stirs up anger.

"The soft answer is the water to quench, grievous words are the oil to stir up the fire. And this is man's natural propensity, to feed rather than to quench, the angry flame. Soft and healing words gain a double victory over ourselves and our brother." ~ C. Bridges

Matthew 18:15-17 ~ [15] "If your brother sins, go and show him his fault in private; if he listens to you, you have won your brother. [16] But if he does not listen to you, take one or two more with you, so that BY THE MOUTH OF TWO OR THREE WITNESSES EVERY FACT MAY BE CONFIRMED. [17] If he refuses to listen to them, tell it to the church; and if he refuses to listen even to the church, let him be to you as a Gentile and a tax collector.

Luke 6:27-28 ~ [27] "But I say to you who hear, love your enemies, do good to those who hate you, [28] bless those who curse you, pray for those who mistreat you.

"The conduct here recommended is beautifully exemplified in the case of our Lord praying for those that crucified Him, and Stephen praying for those who stoned him.

Luke 23:34; Acts 7:60" ~ J. C. Ryle

The act of forgiving is a wonderfully simple act; but it always happens inside a storm of complex emotions. It is the hardest thing in the whole bag of personal relationships. If we can press on through it, we may even achieve reconciliation.

Forgiveness is a process which usually takes time and may need to be repeated. You can have forgiven to the best of your ability only to find unwanted anger in your heart again. Don't let these feelings make you believe you did not truly forgive. Sometimes new feelings come from your subconscious or forgotten memories. Simply repeat the process of forgiveness until such feelings arise no more.

Romans 12:9 ~ [9] Let love be without hypocrisy. Abhor what is evil; cling to what is good.

The question of how to deal with people who have wounded us is more complicated than the question of how to deal with those we have hurt. The Bible teaches that there are times to speak, and times to be silent; times to confront, and times to forbear. How are we to know what to do in a given situation?

When in doubt, we can always seek counsel. We cannot make others responsible for our choices, but we can get insights and ask for prayer from those we trust to help us choose wisely. We alone are responsible for our decisions, but we need not decide alone.

Having sought advice, we can also lay the matter before The One, True Living GOD, YAHWEH. We can ask HIM to show us our own hearts (Psalm 139:23-24). We can ask for Wisdom (James 1:5). We can ask HIM to give us, and the ones we are called to confront, a right spirit and a tender, loving, humble heart.

Now we must make our decision and act on it. Remember, there is no perfection here. We are not The CREATOR, but merely creatures; not infinite, but limited; not infallible, but liable to err. Not sinless creatures but fallen ones.

GOD has not chosen to perfect us at conversion but calls us to grow up into JESUS The CHRIST in all things (Ephesians 4:15). Sin can still put one over on us, but we do not have to let our lack of perfection paralyze us.

Finally, let us not make the mistake of thinking that if we do everything right, we will be loved; but, if we are rejected, we must have done something wrong.

We do not follow the Bible to control the responses of others. We follow the Bible because we have an All-Knowing and All Loving FATHER that robed HIMSELF in flesh to come to Earth, become the Man JESUS The CHRIST to be the propitiation for our sins.

As we follow HIM, many people will respond positively to us; others will not. JESUS "did no sin" (1Peter 2:22) but HE was "despised and rejected of men" (Isaiah 53:3). "The servant is not greater than his lord" (John 15:20). Let us do our best, trust in, and surrender to, JESUS The CHRIST, and commit ourselves "to HIM that judgeth righteously" (1Peter 2:23).

At this time, please consider what you've read and learned, and journal your own personal response to this. This can be of great help in the future to see how you are progressing and changing.

Fear of rejection has always been a major problem for me. That fear made even thinking about working these methods so very painful, so the thought of putting it in print and offering it to others really was difficult!

There are a lot of "programs" and "therapies" out there, and please understand that this is nothing like those programs and totally in opposition to those therapies. YESHUA, JESUS The CHRIST, is The One True Conversion Therapy, and there are no others besides HIM! AMen!!

Programs can 'set you free', yes they can. Ministries can also. Therapies can 'set those seeking freedom free' and even have them believe the lie of same-sex attraction has been conquered. Only The SON, JESUS The CHRIST, can "Make You Free!"

Only The FATHER can reveal to you what HIS intended design is for you. Only HE can reveal what true pure intimacy is while destroying the lies of the enemy like same-sex attraction.

The entirety of these methods, in this order, has been an integral part of the process of discovering who I was intended and Created to be from the very beginning.

If I really want to continue to enjoy Freedom, I simply have to build this pattern into my life. In the past, my pattern had been to avoid people who were angry with me as much as possible.

I'm still in the process of making amends to those I've hurt, and probably will be for many years to come. Most have responded kindly; some needed time to work through their hurts; a few have been unwilling to forgive; one or two would not even hear me.

Whatever the response, I have the Peace that comes from knowing I am doing what I can to rectify my past failures. Some of the people I wounded are now among my most loyal supporters, so I am less alone. I've found that making amends enables me to move on in my life with a clear conscience, unfettered by the past, and that feels good!

Helpful Hints...

Make a list of those to whom you need to make amends as outlined at the beginning of this chapter.

1) In your journal, write what you want to say to the first person on your amends-making list and discuss what you have written. If wise and possible, make an appointment to make amends with that person and discuss the outcome with a brother or sister, or even in your group. Journal what you are learning from all of this and share your findings and feelings with others.

2) Memorize one of the verses you found helpful in this chapter.